Brownies, Blondies
& Bar Cookies

(cover brownies)

1. Peanut Butter Brownie Cups
2. Blueberry Cheesecake Blondies
3. Mocha-Almond Fudge Brownies
4. Laura's #1 Lunch-Box Treats
5. Chocolate Cream Liqueur Brownies
6. Remarkable Raspberry Meringues
7. Best-Ever Buttermilk Brownies
8. German Chocolate Fudgies
9. Pecan-Praline Chocolate Bars

Brownies, Blondies & Bar Cookies

by
Laura Gates & Ann Binney

Illustrations by
Katherine Potter

HPBooks
a division of
PRICE STERN SLOAN
Los Angeles

© 1991 by Laura Gates and Ann Binney
Illustrations © 1991 by Price Stern Sloan, Inc.
Published by HPBooks, a division of Price Stern Sloan, Inc.
11150 Olympic Boulevard, Suite 650
Los Angeles, California, 90064

Printed in U.S.A.
9 8 7 6 5 4 3 2 1

Gates, Laura.
    Brownies, blondies and bar cookies/by Laura Gates and Ann Binney.
        p.   cm.
    Includes index.
        1. Brownies (Cookery)   I. Binney, Ann.   II. Title.
TX771.G37   1991
641.8'653—dc20   91-8928
                                                            CIP

This book is printed on acid free-paper.

Dedication

To our Moms–
Without whom this book would not be possible.

Acknowledgments

Thanks to all our tried and true taste-testers, friends, family and co-workers. Your always-hungry stomachs, your never-lying taste buds, and your endless support during the writing of this book are greatly appreciated. And a special thanks to Nick for believing in us and Corrine, Beth, Bret and Jeanette for putting up with us.

Table of Contents

Introduction

We've written this book out of life-long love affairs with desserts. Memories of surreptitiously sneaking into the cookie jar after hours, savoring snack-time milk and cookies with friends and baking sweets with Mom are vivid in both our minds. Our early childhood interest in baking and baked goods grew into a teenage hobby and later an adult passion. Here's a book filled with our favorite recipes so you can bring the pleasures of fresh-baked goods to your family and friends.

Brownies are an American tradition. Really a bar cookie in chocolate wraps, the brownie has broken into a realm of greatness all its own. Brownies have long been favorites at bake sales, county fairs, soda fountains and in lunch boxes. After all, who can resist a uniquely satisfying bite of deep, dark chocolate brownie filled with nuts, topped with fudge frosting and capped off with an ice-cold glass of milk? We've taken the traditional brownie, presented it in all its wonderful cakey, gooey variations, and then gone beyond the ordinary with a unique collection of gourmet varieties. Delicate liqueurs, cream cheese, white chocolate and fresh fruits and nuts are just a few of the additions that turn the marvelously mundane chocolate square into a new taste sensation!

You may wonder, "What's a blondie?" Well, simply put, it's an un-chocolate brownie. Like their dark-colored relatives, blondies can be either chewy or tending toward cakelike, though never crunchy like a cookie or flakey like cake. Buttery rich and full of brown sugar, the blondie recipes given here creatively combine a range of delectable ingredients warranting, lo' and behold, a chapter all to themselves! Whether citrus-spiced or cherry-bombed, these blondies are sure to win over even the most die-hard chocoholics!

Variety is the spice of life, and bar cookies are certainly well-seasoned! Running the gamut from gooey to tartlike, breakfast bites to after-dinner delights, the bar cookies presented here come fudge-frosted, fruit-flecked and meringue-topped. The possibilities are many, the outcome always the same: they're mouth-wateringly good morning, noon or night!

Though the ingredients and method may vary, your cookie-making efforts will guarantee one result: a great-tasting confection that's sure to satisfy every sweet tooth in your house. So put away your pastry bags, your candy thermometers, your two-page recipes...all you'll need here is standard kitchen stuff–bowls, saucepans, sifters, spoons and the like. Go ahead, try your hand at these recipes, and in just minutes, you'll have the fragrant aroma of home-baked goods wafting from your oven.

To insure unbeatable brownie, blondie and bar cookie treats, we've outlined some of the key ingredients, utensils and a few essential pointers that will be helpful when making the recipes in this book. Read them over before you begin a recipe, refer to them as necessary and you're sure to bake the best batch possible!

Equipment

Glass Pans: Normally when using glass pans, you may need to decrease your oven temperature by as much as 25 degrees and/or reduce cooking time to prevent too-rapid baking. However, the recipes in this book were created to be baked in glass or ceramic pans and thus, the oven temperature and cooking times reflect this.

Aluminum Pans: If you use aluminum baking pans, follow the oven temperatures and times indicated and test for doneness as specified. The more used and darkened an aluminum pan is, the better the heat is distributed, thus achieving better baking results. Season a brand-new pan by washing it in warm, soapy water and drying it thoroughly. Rub the bottom and sides with oil and bake empty in a 425-degree oven for 20 minutes.

Pan Size: Pan size is very important, and substitutions could have a major effect on the finished brownie or bar cookie. We strongly recommend you use the pan size indicated. When in doubt, measure the pan.

Ingredients

Butter/Margarine: Margarine can be substituted in most recipes. However, if you desire a rich, buttery flavor, we suggest using real butter or half butter, half margarine. Lightly salted butter should be used to enhance flavor unless otherwise specified.

Chocolate: Always use real chocolate! Whether the recipe calls for unsweetened, semisweet or milk chocolate, do not substitute imitation chocolate for the real thing. Semisweet chocolate is another term for bittersweet chocolate, which should not be confused with bitter or unsweetened chocolate or cocoa powder, which has no sugar in it. When a recipe calls for melting chocolate, always carefully melt over low heat, stirring frequently to avoid burning. If chocolate becomes lumpy when melted, smooth out by adding flavorless vegetable oil or boiling water, one teaspoon at a time, until chocolate reaches desired consistency.

White Chocolate: Though it is not technically considered chocolate since it contains no brown chocolate liquor, white chocolate lends a delicious, unique flavor to brownies, blondies and bar cookies. It consists of cocoa, butter, milk, sugar and flavorings. Beware when melting white chocolate as it burns easily. Stir constantly when melting.

Eggs: All the recipes in this book have been tested with U.S. Grade AA large eggs. We suggest you use Grade AA large eggs or extra large eggs. However, if you only have small eggs, use two small eggs to one large egg or use one small egg plus four tablespoons of water or milk.

Egg Whites: When making meringues, it is better to separate eggs when cold. However, allow egg whites to warm to room temperature before beating. Remember, the slightest bit of egg yolk in egg whites can prevent them from peaking.

Extracts: Many of the recipes in this book call for extracts such as vanilla, almond, etc. We strongly recommend that you always use pure extracts as opposed to artificial flavorings. Pure extracts will give your baked goods a rich, true flavor.

Flour: Always use the type of flour specified in the recipe. Never substitute cake flour or self-rising flour for all-purpose flour. Also, unbleached flour is generally more nutritious and better tasting than bleached flour.

Fruit: Whenever possible, use fresh, ripe fruit. However, if a particular fruit is not in season, frozen fruit can be used. Always try to get fruit that is not sweetened or packaged in syrup. Using unsweetened frozen fruit will result in a fresher tasting dessert.

Nuts: Unless specifically indicated in the recipe, as in the recipe for Pecan-Praline Chocolate Bars, nuts can be interchanged or omitted as desired. Shelled nuts can spoil rapidly and therefore should be stored in the freezer or in airtight vacuum-sealed bags.

Oil: Any flavorless vegetable oil can be used.

Shortening: Vegetable shortening or butter can be used for greasing the baking pans. We also find the non-stick spray to be convenient, not to mention, lower in calories! (But then again, these recipes are far from low-cal!)

Sweetened Condensed Milk: Do not substitute evaporated milk for sweetened condensed milk. Evaporated milk does not contain sugar; sweetened condensed milk contains 40–45% sugar.

Storage

Always cool brownies or bar cookies completely before storing. They can be stored in their original baking pans, tightly covered with foil or plastic wrap for up to five days.

Brownies and bar cookies can also be frozen up to one month. Before freezing, cool completely. Wrap the cut brownies or bar cookies in moisture-proof containers or airtight freezer bags.

Frozen brownies or bar cookies can be defrosted, unwrapped or in their package, in approximately thirty minutes. If desired, thawed brownies or bar cookies can be warmed in a 300F(150C) oven for about five minutes, or microwaved on low or medium setting for about one minute, for a just-baked goodness.

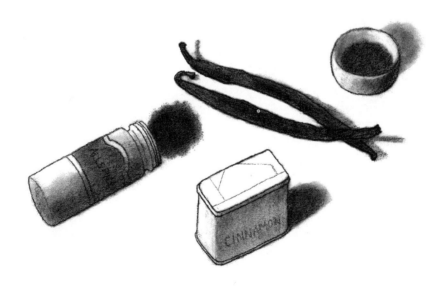

❖

Chapter One

Traditional Brownies

❖

Guaranteed to please brownie lovers of all kinds, here's a batch of recipes for fudgelike, cakelike and chewy, chocolate favorites. Although basic brownie ingredients make these recipes traditional, they are far from ordinary.

Milk Chocolate Dream Brownies

A lighter version of a traditional semisweet chocolate brownie that tastes just as great! Any milk chocolate candy bar can be used in this recipe.

4 OUNCES MILK CHOCOLATE

1/2 CUP BUTTER OR MARGARINE

2 EGGS

3/4 CUP SUGAR

1 TEASPOON VANILLA EXTRACT

3/4 CUP ALL-PURPOSE FLOUR

1/2 CUP CHOPPED WALNUTS OR PECANS
   (OPTIONAL)

Preheat oven to 350F (175C). Grease a 9-inch-square baking pan. In a small saucepan over low heat, melt chocolate and butter or margarine, stirring until smooth. Remove from heat and let cool to lukewarm. In a large bowl, beat eggs and sugar until light and frothy. Add vanilla and melted chocolate mixture. Add flour and beat until blended and smooth. Fold in nuts, if desired. Spread batter into prepared pan and bake 25 minutes or until a wooden pick inserted in center comes out moist. Do not overbake. Set on a wire rack and cool in pan. Cut in 16 to 25 squares.

Chocolate Pudding Brownies

Chocolate pudding mix makes these moist brownies mouth-wateringly delicious !

3/4 CUP BUTTER OR MARGARINE

1 CUP SUGAR

1-1/2 TEASPOONS VANILLA EXTRACT

3 EGGS

1/2 CUP UNSWEETENED COCOA POWDER

1/2 TEASPOON BAKING POWDER

1 CUP ALL-PURPOSE FLOUR

1/2 CUP CHOCOLATE (OR CHOCOLATE
   FUDGE) PUDDING AND PIE FILLING MIX*

1/2 CUP MILK CHOCOLATE CHIPS

* DO NOT USE INSTANT PUDDING MIX

Preheat oven to 350F (175C). Grease a 9-inch-square baking pan. In a small saucepan over low heat, melt butter or margarine, stirring until smooth. Remove from heat and let cool to lukewarm. In a large bowl, combine melted butter or margarine and sugar and beat with a wire whisk until blended. Beat in vanilla and eggs. Add cocoa, baking powder, flour and pudding mix and blend well. Fold in chocolate chips. Spread batter into prepared pan and bake 25 to 30 minutes, or until a wooden pick inserted in center comes out clean. Set on a wire rack and cool in pan. Cut in 25 squares.

Variation: Substitute 1/2 cup peanut butter chips for 1/2 cup milk chocolate chips.

Cake Classics

To make these delicious cakelike brownies fancier, frost with your favorite frosting.

1-1/2 CUPS ALL-PURPOSE FLOUR
1/2 TEASPOON BAKING SODA
3 TABLESPOONS UNSWEETENED COCOA
    POWDER
1/2 CUP BUTTER OR MARGARINE,
    SOFTENED
1-1/2 CUPS PACKED DARK BROWN SUGAR
1 EGG
1/2 CUP MILK
1/2 CUP HOT WATER
1/2 CUP CHOPPED WALNUTS OR PECANS
    (OPTIONAL)

Preheat oven to 350F (175C). Grease an 8-inch-square baking pan. In a small bowl, combine flour, baking soda and cocoa. Set aside. In a large bowl, beat together butter or margarine and brown sugar until light and fluffy. Gradually add egg and milk and mix well. Add flour mixture alternately with hot water, and mix until smooth. Fold in nuts, if desired. Spread batter into prepared pan and bake 25 to 30 minutes, or until a wooden pick inserted in center comes out clean. Set on a wire rack and cool in pan. Cut in 16 squares. Frost, if desired.

Chocolate Syrup Brownies

For a real chocolate treat, top these fudgy squares with additional chocolate syrup just before serving.

1-1/4 CUPS ALL-PURPOSE FLOUR

1/4 TEASPOON BAKING SODA

1/2 CUP BUTTER OR MARGARINE,
   SOFTENED

1 CUP SUGAR

2 EGGS

1 TEASPOON VANILLA EXTRACT

3/4 CUP CHOCOLATE SYRUP

1/2 CUP CHOPPED WALNUTS OR PECANS
   (OPTIONAL)

Preheat oven to 350F (175C). Grease a 13" x 9" baking dish. In a small bowl, combine flour and baking soda. Set aside. In a large bowl, beat together butter or margarine and sugar until light and fluffy. Add eggs and vanilla. Add flour mixture to egg mixture alternately with chocolate syrup, beating until smooth. Fold in nuts, if desired. Spread batter into prepared pan and bake 40 to 45 minutes or until a wooden pick inserted in center comes out barely moist. Set on a wire rack and cool in pan. Cut in 24 squares.

Either-Or Brownies

Both chewy and cakelike brownie fans will love this fudgy, yet slightly cakelike version.

4 OUNCES UNSWEETENED CHOCOLATE

1 CUP ALL-PURPOSE FLOUR

3/4 TEASPOON BAKING POWDER

4 EGGS

1-2/3 CUPS SUGAR

2 TEASPOONS VANILLA EXTRACT

2/3 CUP VEGETABLE OIL

1 CUP CHOPPED WALNUTS OR PECANS
   (OPTIONAL)

Preheat oven to 375F (175C). Grease a 13" x 9" baking pan. In a small saucepan over low heat, melt chocolate, stirring until smooth. Remove from heat and let cool to lukewarm. In a small bowl, combine flour and baking powder. Set aside. In a large bowl, beat eggs until thick and light in color. Gradually beat in sugar until blended. Add vanilla, oil and chocolate and mix well. Stir in flour mixture. Fold in nuts, if desired. Spread batter into prepared pan and bake 25 to 30 minutes, or until a wooden pick inserted 1-1/2 inches from center comes out clean. Set on a wire rack and cool in pan. Cut in 32 squares.

The Original All-American Fudge Brownie

Just the way Mom used to make them…filled with chocolate and nuts,
this most popular of fudge brownie recipes has stood the test of time.

2 OUNCES UNSWEETENED CHOCOLATE

1/2 CUP BUTTER OR MARGARINE

2 EGGS

1 CUP SUGAR

1 TABLESPOON VANILLA EXTRACT

1/2 CUP ALL-PURPOSE FLOUR

1 CUP NUTS (OPTIONAL)

Preheat oven to 350F (175C). Grease a 9-inch-square baking pan. In a small saucepan over low heat, melt chocolate and butter or margarine, stirring until smooth. Remove from heat and let cool to lukewarm. In a large bowl, beat eggs, sugar and vanilla. Beat in cooled chocolate mixture. Add flour, beating 50 strokes by hand. Fold in nuts, if desired. Spread batter into prepared pan and bake 18 to 22 minutes, or until a wooden pick inserted 1-1/2 inches from center comes out barely moist. Set on a wire rack and cool in pan. Cut in 25 squares.

Annie's Best Brownies

Extra fudgy, extra yummy brownies. Moist, chocolatey and delicious!

2 OUNCES UNSWEETENED CHOCOLATE

1/4 CUP SEMISWEET CHOCOLATE CHIPS

1/2 CUP BUTTER OR MARGARINE

3/4 CUP ALL-PURPOSE FLOUR

1/2 CUP UNSWEETENED COCOA POWDER

1/2 TEASPOON BAKING POWDER

1 CUP PACKED DARK BROWN SUGAR

1/2 CUP GRANULATED SUGAR

1/4 CUP VEGETABLE OIL

1 EGG

1/3 CUP WATER

1 TABLESPOON VANILLA EXTRACT

1 CUP CHOPPED NUTS (OPTIONAL)

Preheat oven to 350F (175C). Grease a 9-inch-square baking pan. In a small saucepan over low heat, melt unsweetened chocolate, semisweet chocolate chips and butter or margarine, stirring until smooth. Remove from heat and let cool to lukewarm. In a small bowl, sift flour, cocoa and baking powder. Set aside. In a large bowl, combine sugars. Stir in cooled chocolate mixture, blending well. In a small bowl, whisk oil, egg, water and vanilla. Add to chocolate mixture, beating thoroughly. Stir in flour mixture, beating 50 strokes by hand. Fold in nuts, if desired. Spread batter into prepared pan and bake 18 to 22 minutes, or until a wooden pick inserted in center comes out barely moist. Set on a wire rack and cool in pan. Cut in 25 squares.

Semisweet Squares

Luscious, semisweet squares made with semisweet baking chocolate or traditional chocolate chips.

8 OUNCES SEMISWEET CHOCOLATE (OR 1-
    1/4 CUPS SEMISWEET CHOCOLATE
    CHIPS)
1/2 CUP UNSALTED BUTTER OR
    MARGARINE
2 EGGS
2/3 CUP SUGAR
2 TEASPOONS VANILLA EXTRACT
1/4 CUP ALL-PURPOSE FLOUR
1 CUP CHOPPED WALNUTS (OPTIONAL)
POWDERED SUGAR

Preheat oven to 375F (190C). Grease a 9-inch-square baking pan. In a small saucepan over low heat, melt chocolate and butter or margarine, stirring until smooth. Remove from heat and let cool to lukewarm. In a medium bowl, beat eggs until frothy. Gradually add sugar and beat until thick and light in color, about 8 minutes. Beat in vanilla. Pour cooled chocolate mixture into eggs, gently folding in, keeping mixture as light and airy as possible. Fold in flour, then nuts, if desired. Spread batter into prepared pan, and bake 25 to 30 minutes, or until wooden pick inserted in center comes out barely moist. Set on a wire rack and cool in pan. Dust with powdered sugar. Cut in 16 to 20 squares.

Fudge Cake Brownies

Absolutely delicious! Cider vinegar enhances the chocolate flavor in these moist, cakelike brownies.

4-1/2 OUNCES UNSWEETENED CHOCOLATE

1/2 CUP BUTTER OR MARGARINE,
   SOFTENED

3/4 CUP GRANULATED SUGAR

2/3 CUP PACKED DARK BROWN SUGAR

1/3 CUP SWEETENED CONDENSED MILK

2 EGGS

2 TEASPOONS VANILLA EXTRACT

1/2 TABLESPOON CIDER VINEGAR

1 CUP SIFTED ALL-PURPOSE FLOUR

1 CUP CHOPPED WALNUTS OR PECANS
   (OPTIONAL)

POWDERED SUGAR

Preheat oven to 375F (190C). Grease a 9-inch-square baking pan. In a small saucepan over low heat, melt chocolate, stirring until smooth. Remove from heat and let cool to lukewarm. In a large bowl, cream butter or margarine and granulated sugar. Add brown sugar and beat until creamy. Whisk condensed milk and eggs together, then beat into sugar mixture. Beat in vanilla, vinegar and cooled chocolate. Stir in flour by hand, beating 50 strokes. Fold in nuts, if desired. Spread batter into prepared pan and bake 30 to 35 minutes, or until a wooden pick inserted in center comes out barely moist. Set on a wire rack and cool in pan. Dust with powdered sugar. Cut in 16 to 25 squares.

Best-Ever Buttermilk Brownies

*Cool and creamy buttermilk in the batter and frosting
makes these deliciously rich, cakelike brownies extra moist.*

1 CUP UNSALTED BUTTER OR MARGARINE

1 CUP WATER

5 HEAPING TABLESPOONS UNSWEETENED
   COCOA POWDER

2 CUPS SUGAR

2 CUPS ALL-PURPOSE FLOUR

1 TEASPOON BAKING SODA

1/2 CUP BUTTERMILK

2 EGGS

1 TABLESPOON VANILLA EXTRACT

1 TEASPOON ALMOND EXTRACT

1 TEASPOON GRATED LEMON PEEL

1 TEASPOON LEMON JUICE

CHOPPED NUTS (OPTIONAL)

❖

CHOCOLATE BUTTERMILK ICING

1/2 CUP UNSALTED BUTTER OR
   MARGARINE

4 TABLESPOONS BUTTERMILK

5 HEAPING TABLESPOONS UNSWEETENED
   COCOA POWDER

1 TEASPOON VANILLA EXTRACT

2 CUPS POWDERED SUGAR

Preheat oven to 350F (175C). Grease 13" x 9" pan. In a medium saucepan over medium heat, melt butter or margarine. Stir in water and cocoa and whisk until smooth and satiny. Remove from heat and let cool to lukewarm. In a medium bowl, combine sugar, flour and baking soda. Add cocoa mixture, buttermilk, eggs, vanilla, almond extract, lemon peel and lemon juice and blend well. Fold in nuts, if desired. Pour batter into prepared pan and bake 20 to 25 minutes, or until wooden pick inserted in center comes out barely moist. Set on a wire rack and cool in pan. Prepare Chocolate Buttermilk Icing. Spread icing generously over brownies. Sprinkle with nuts, if desired. Refrigerate at least one hour. Cut in 32 squares.

Chocolate Buttermilk Icing

In a medium saucepan over medium heat, melt butter or margarine. Add buttermilk and cocoa and blend until smooth and creamy. Bring to a boil, stirring constantly, and boil for 1 minute. Remove from heat and stir in vanilla. Cool slightly. Place powdered sugar in a large bowl. Gradually add chocolate mixture, beating with an electric mixer until thick and smooth; do not overbeat.

Deluxe Chocolate Brownies

Rich, delectable fudge brownies destined to be crowd pleasers.

2/3 CUP BUTTER OR MARGARINE
5 OUNCES UNSWEETENED CHOCOLATE
1-3/4 CUPS SUGAR
2 TEASPOONS VANILLA EXTRACT
2 EGGS
1/4 CUP WATER
1 CUP ALL-PURPOSE FLOUR
1 CUP SEMISWEET CHOCOLATE CHIPS
1 CUP CHOPPED NUTS (OPTIONAL)
POWDERED SUGAR

Preheat oven to 350F (175C). Grease a 9-inch-square baking pan. In a small saucepan over low heat, melt butter or margarine and chocolate, stirring until smooth. Remove from heat and let cool to lukewarm. In a large bowl, beat sugar, vanilla, eggs and water on high speed for 5 minutes. Beat in chocolate mixture, blending thoroughly. Stir in flour by hand, beating 50 strokes. Fold in chocolate chips and nuts, if desired. Spread batter into prepared pan and bake 40 to 45 minutes, or until a wooden pick inserted in center comes out barely moist and brownies begin to pull away from sides of pan. Set on a wire rack and cool in pan. Dust with powdered sugar. Cut in 25 squares.

Cocoa Brownies

Simple and sweet… the perfect companion to a glass of ice-cold milk.

1 CUP SUGAR

1/2 CUP BUTTER OR MARGARINE,
   SOFTENED

2 TEASPOONS VANILLA EXTRACT

2 EGGS

2/3 CUP ALL-PURPOSE FLOUR

1/2 CUP UNSWEETENED COCOA POWDER

1/2 TEASPOON BAKING POWDER

1/2 CUP CHOPPED NUTS (OPTIONAL)

Preheat oven to 350F (175C). Grease an 8-inch-square baking pan. In a medium bowl, beat sugar, butter or margarine, vanilla and eggs until creamy. Sift in flour, cocoa and baking powder and beat 50 strokes or until thoroughly blended. Fold in nuts, if desired. Spread batter into prepared pan and bake 25 to 30 minutes, or until a wooden pick inserted in center comes out barely moist. Set on a wire rack and cool in pan. Cut in 16 squares.

---❖---

Chapter Two

Gourmet Brownies

---❖---

Fasten your aprons and prepare your taste buds for a trip into the new world of brownies. A gourmet's delight, these recipes run the brownie gamut–featuring everything from mint to macadamia nuts, raspberries to raisins!

Fig Fabulous Brownies

*With roots in the classic newton, these newfangled fig treats are sure to please
with a yummy fig spread nestled between fudgy brownie layers and topped with orange glaze.*

FIG FILLING

2 CUPS FINELY CHOPPED DRIED, STEMMED
    FIGS (ABOUT 8 OUNCES)

1/2 CUP WATER

3 TABLESPOONS DARK BROWN SUGAR

1 TABLESPOON GRATED ORANGE PEEL

1 TABLESPOON FRESH ORANGE JUICE

1/8 TEASPOON GROUND ALLSPICE

❖

FUDGE BROWNIE

2 OUNCES UNSWEETENED CHOCOLATE

1/3 CUP SEMISWEET CHOCOLATE CHIPS

1/4 CUP BUTTER OR MARGARINE

1 CUP GRANULATED SUGAR

1/4 CUP PLUS 2 TABLESPOONS PACKED
    DARK BROWN SUGAR

2 EGGS

1 TABLESPOON VANILLA EXTRACT

2/3 CUP SIFTED ALL-PURPOSE FLOUR

❖

ORANGE GLAZE

3/4 CUP POWDERED SUGAR

1 TABLESPOON ORANGE LIQUEUR

1 TABLESPOON FRESH ORANGE JUICE

Fig Filling

In a large saucepan, combine figs, water, brown sugar, orange peel, orange juice and allspice. Bring to a boil, stirring to dissolve sugar. Reduce heat to low, cover and simmer, stirring occasionally, about 8 minutes, or until all liquid is absorbed and mixture begins to thicken. Remove from heat and cool slightly. In a blender, process fig mixture until it resembles a thick paste. Set aside.

Fudge Brownie

Preheat oven to 325F (165C). Grease a 9-inch-square baking pan. In a small saucepan, melt unsweetened chocolate, semisweet chocolate chips and butter or margarine over low heat, stirring until smooth. Cool to lukewarm. In a large bowl, combine sugars. Whisk eggs and vanilla together and add to sugars, stirring until thoroughly blended. Stir in cooled chocolate mixture. Stir flour into chocolate mixture, beating 50 strokes by hand. Spread half of batter into prepared pan. Top with fig mixture. Spoon remaining batter over fig mixture and spread gently. Cover tightly with foil. Bake 15 minutes. Remove foil and bake 30 minutes or until a wooden pick inserted in center comes out with moist crumbs attached. Set on a wire rack and cool in pan. Prepare Orange Glaze. Cut in 25 squares, leave in pan. Spread glaze evenly over cut brownies, allowing glaze to seep into cracks and crevices. Let stand, until glaze sets, about 20 minutes.

Orange Glaze

Mix all ingredients in small bowl.

Mocha-Almond Fudge Brownies

*Studded with white chocolate chips, there's really only
one word to describe these rich, coffee-almond brownies—delectable!*

3/4 CUP BUTTER OR MARGARINE

2 OUNCES UNSWEETENED CHOCOLATE

1/3 CUP SEMISWEET CHOCOLATE CHIPS

1 CUP PACKED DARK BROWN SUGAR

1/2 CUP GRANULATED SUGAR

2 TEASPOONS VANILLA EXTRACT

1 TEASPOON ALMOND EXTRACT

1 TABLESPOON INSTANT COFFEE POWDER

1/3 CUP BOILING WATER

1 EGG

3/4 CUP ALL-PURPOSE FLOUR

1/2 CUP UNSWEETENED COCOA POWDER

1/4 TEASPOON BAKING SODA

1/4 TEASPOON BAKING POWDER

1 CUP WHITE CHOCOLATE CHIPS

POWDERED SUGAR

Preheat oven to 350F (175C). Grease a 9-inch-square baking pan. In a small saucepan over low heat, melt butter or margarine, unsweetened chocolate and semisweet chocolate chips, stirring until smooth. Remove from heat and let cool to lukewarm. In a large bowl, combine sugars. Add cooled chocolate mixture and vanilla and almond extract. In a glass measuring cup, dissolve coffee powder in boiling water and let cool slightly, then whisk in egg. Blend into chocolate mixture, stirring until smooth and velvety. Sift together flour, cocoa, baking soda and baking powder and stir into chocolate mixture, beating 50 strokes by hand. Fold in white chocolate chips. Spread batter into prepared pan and bake 30 to 35 minutes, or until a wooden pick inserted in center comes out barely moist. Set on a wire rack and cool in pan. Dust with powdered sugar. Cut in 25 squares.

Chocolate-Raspberry Cheesecake Brownies

*Raspberry and chocolate—always a winning combination—team
up in these sinfully delicious chocolate-cheesecake dessert treats.*

1/2 CUP BUTTER OR MARGARINE

2 OUNCES UNSWEETENED CHOCOLATE

1/4 CUP SEMISWEET CHOCOLATE CHIPS

3/4 CUP ALL-PURPOSE FLOUR

1/2 CUP UNSWEETENED COCOA POWDER

1/4 TEASPOON BAKING SODA

1/4 TEASPOON BAKING POWDER

1 CUP PACKED DARK BROWN SUGAR

1/4 CUP GRANULATED SUGAR

1 TABLESPOON VANILLA EXTRACT

1 EGG

1/3 CUP RASPBERRY SCHNAPPS

2 TABLESPOONS RASPBERRY JAM

3/4 CUP CHOPPED WALNUTS

1 CUP SEMISWEET CHOCOLATE CHIPS

❖

RASPBERRY CHEESECAKE TOPPING

8 OUNCES CREAM CHEESE, SOFTENED

1 EGG

1/3 CUP SUGAR

1 TEASPOON VANILLA EXTRACT

2 TABLESPOONS RASPBERRY JAM

Preheat oven to 350F (175C). Grease a 13" x 9" baking pan. In a small saucepan over low heat, melt butter or margarine, unsweetened chocolate and semisweet chocolate chips, stirring until smooth. Remove from heat and let cool to lukewarm. Sift flour, cocoa, baking soda and baking powder into a small bowl. Set aside. In a large bowl, combine sugars. Add cooled chocolate mixture and vanilla. Whisk together egg, schnapps and jam and blend into chocolate mixture. Stir in dry ingredients, beating 50 strokes. Spread batter into prepared pan and set aside. Prepare Raspberry Cheesecake Topping. Spread topping evenly over brownie mixture. Sprinkle walnuts and chocolate chips over cheesecake topping. Bake 25 to 30 minutes, or until a wooden pick inserted in center comes out barely moist and cheesecake topping is golden and is set but soft. Set on a wire rack and cool in pan. Refrigerate overnight. Cut in 16 to 25 squares.

Raspberry Cheesecake Topping
In a small bowl, beat all ingredients until smooth and creamy.

Variation: Substitute 1/3 cup water and 1-1/2 teaspoons raspberry extract for 1/3 cup raspberry schnapps.

Cream Cheese Treasures

These tasty cream cheese bites are topped with nuts, coconut and chocolate chips. Delicious!

1 CUP BUTTER OR MARGARINE

3 OUNCES UNSWEETENED CHOCOLATE

3/4 CUP SEMISWEET CHOCOLATE CHIPS

1-1/4 CUPS ALL-PURPOSE FLOUR

1/2 CUP UNSWEETENED COCOA POWDER

1/4 TEASPOON BAKING SODA

1/4 TEASPOON BAKING POWDER

1 CUP PACKED DARK BROWN SUGAR

1/2 CUP GRANULATED SUGAR

1 TABLESPOON VANILLA EXTRACT

1 EGG

1/2 CUP COLD WATER

1 CUP SEMISWEET CHOCOLATE CHIPS

1 CUP CHOPPED WALNUTS

1 CUP FLAKED COCONUT

❖

CREAM CHEESE TOPPING

8 OUNCES CREAM CHEESE, SOFTENED

1 EGG

1/2 CUP SUGAR

1 TEASPOON VANILLA EXTRACT

1 TABLESPOON GRATED ORANGE PEEL

Preheat oven to 350F (175C). Grease a 13" x 9" baking pan. In a small saucepan over low heat, melt butter or margarine, unsweetened chocolate and semisweet chocolate chips, stirring until smooth. Remove from heat and let cool to lukewarm. Sift flour, cocoa, baking soda and baking powder into a small bowl. Set aside. In a large bowl, combine sugars. Add cooled chocolate mixture and vanilla. Whisk together egg and water and blend into chocolate mixture. Stir in flour mixture by hand, beating 50 strokes. Spread batter into prepared pan and set aside. Prepare Cream Cheese Topping. Spread evenly over brownie layer. In a small bowl, combine semisweet chocolate chips, nuts and coconut. Sprinkle evenly over cheesecake topping. Bake 25 to 30 minutes, or until a wooden pick inserted in center comes out barely moist and cheesecake topping is golden and is set but soft. Set on a wire rack and cool in pan. Refrigerate overnight. Cut in 30 squares.

Cream Cheese Topping
In a medium bowl, beat together cream cheese, egg, sugar, vanilla and orange peel until well blended.

Mint Condition Brownies

Mint chocolate chips and crème de cacao are the key to these refreshing, rich choco-mint brownies.

FUDGE BROWNIE

1/2 CUP UNSALTED BUTTER OR
    MARGARINE

1 CUP MINT CHOCOLATE CHIPS

2 OUNCES UNSWEETENED CHOCOLATE

2 TABLESPOONS CRÈME DE CACAO
    LIQUEUR (OR 2 TABLESPOONS
    CHOCOLATE SYRUP)

2 TABLESPOONS WHIPPING CREAM

2 TEASPOONS INSTANT ESPRESSO
    POWDER (OR INSTANT COFFEE)

1 CUP SUGAR

1 EGG

1 CUP ALL-PURPOSE FLOUR

❖

GREEN MINT FROSTING

1/2 CUP MINT CHOCOLATE CHIPS

1 OUNCE UNSWEETENED CHOCOLATE

5 TABLESPOONS UNSALTED BUTTER OR
    MARGARINE, SOFTENED

❖

MINT CHOCOLATE GLAZE

1/2 CUP BUTTER OR MARGARINE,
    SOFTENED

2 CUPS POWDERED SUGAR

1/4 CUP GREEN CRÈME DE MENTHE
    LIQUEUR

Fudge Brownie

Preheat oven to 350F (175C). Grease a 9-inch-square baking pan. In a small saucepan over low heat, melt butter or margarine, mint chocolate chips and unsweetened chocolate, stirring frequently to avoid burning. Remove from heat and let cool to lukewarm. In a small cup, mix crème de cacao liqueur, cream and espresso powder. Set aside. In a large bowl, beat sugar and egg until frothy. Fold in coffee mixture, then melted chocolate. Stir in flour by hand, beating 50 strokes. Spread batter into prepared pan and bake 25 minutes, or until a wooden pick inserted in center comes out barely moist. Set on a wire rack and cool in pan. Prepare Green Mint Frosting. Frost cooled brownies and refrigerate while preparing Mint Chocolate Glaze. Spread glaze over frosted brownies. Refrigerate at least 4 hours before cutting. Cut in 24 squares. Store in refrigerator.

Green Mint Frosting

In a small bowl, cream all ingredients.

Mint Chocolate Glaze

In a small saucepan over low heat, melt all ingredients, stirring until smooth. Remove from heat and let cool to room temperature.

Variation: Substitute 1 teaspoon peppermint extract, 2 to 3 drops green food coloring and 4 tablespoons milk for crème de menthe liqueur.

Chocolate Cheesecake Dream Bars

*Fudgy, creamy… dreamy! This incredible chocolatey brownie is finished
off with luscious chocolate cheesecake topping and semisweet chocolate curls.*

4 OUNCES UNSWEETENED CHOCOLATE

6 TABLESPOONS UNSALTED BUTTER OR
MARGARINE

3/4 CUP ALL-PURPOSE FLOUR

1/4 TEASPOON BAKING SODA

1 TEASPOON INSTANT COFFEE POWDER

2 TEASPOONS WATER

2 TEASPOONS VANILLA EXTRACT

1/2 TABLESPOON CIDER VINEGAR

1 EGG

1/3 CUP BUTTERMILK

1-1/2 CUPS SUGAR

3-1/2 OUNCES MILK OR SEMISWEET
CHOCOLATE, GRATED INTO CURLS

❖

CHOCOLATE CHEESECAKE TOPPING

2 OUNCES UNSWEETENED CHOCOLATE

2 TABLESPOONS ALMOND-FLAVORED
LIQUEUR (OR 2 TABLESPOONS WATER
AND 1 TEASPOON ALMOND EXTRACT)

1 TEASPOON VANILLA EXTRACT

8 OUNCES CREAM CHEESE, SOFTENED

3/4 CUP SUGAR

1 EGG

Preheat oven to 325F (165C). Grease a 9-inch-square baking pan. In a small saucepan over low heat, melt chocolate and butter or margarine, stirring until smooth. Remove from heat and let cool to lukewarm. In a small bowl, combine flour and baking soda. Set aside. In a small cup, mix coffee powder, water, vanilla and vinegar. In a large bowl, beat egg, buttermilk and sugar. Add coffee mixture and mix well. Fold in melted chocolate, then flour mixture. Spread batter into prepared pan and bake 35 minutes, or until a wooden pick inserted in center comes out moist and top is dry and cracked. Set on a wire rack. Maintain oven temperature. Prepare Chocolate Cheesecake Topping. Pour topping over brownies and return to oven. Bake until topping moves just slightly in the center when shaken, about 10 minutes. Set on a wire rack and cool in pan. Grate milk or semisweet chocolate into small curls and sprinkle over cooled brownies. Refrigerate overnight. Cut in 25 squares. Store in refrigerator.

Chocolate Cheesecake Topping

In a small saucepan over low heat, melt chocolate. Remove from heat and stir in liqueur and vanilla. In a small bowl, blend cream cheese and sugar until smooth. Add chocolate mixture and egg, and blend just until combined.

Apricot Fudge Club Squares

A classic pair–apricot and chocolate–debut in these sophisticated fruit treats.

3 OUNCES UNSWEETENED CHOCOLATE

6 TABLESPOONS UNSALTED BUTTER OR
  MARGARINE

1 CUP ALL-PURPOSE FLOUR

3 TABLESPOONS UNSWEETENED COCOA
  POWDER

1/4 TEASPOON BAKING SODA

1-1/2 CUPS GRANULATED SUGAR

3 TABLESPOONS POWDERED SUGAR

2 EGGS

1/3 CUP PLUS 2 TABLESPOONS
  APRICOT JAM

1-1/2 TEASPOONS RED WINE VINEGAR

❖

APRICOT GLAZE

2 OUNCES SEMISWEET CHOCOLATE

3 TABLESPOONS APRICOT JAM

2 TABLESPOONS UNSALTED BUTTER OR
  MARGARINE

1/4 TEASPOON RED WINE VINEGAR

Preheat oven to 325F (165C). Grease a 9-inch-square baking pan. In a small saucepan over low heat, melt chocolate and butter or margarine, stirring until smooth. Remove from heat and let cool to lukewarm. In a small bowl, sift flour, cocoa and baking soda. Set aside. In a large bowl, beat sugars and eggs until pale yellow. Add 2 tablespoons jam and 1/2 teaspoon vinegar and beat 1 minute. Fold in melted chocolate mixture. Add dry ingredients and mix thoroughly. Spread batter into prepared pan and bake 30 to 35 minutes, or until a wooden pick inserted in center comes out moist. Set pan on a wire rack and allow to cool in pan. In a small bowl, mix remaining 1/3 cup jam and remaining 1 teaspoon vinegar and spread over hot brownies. Cool completely. Prepare Apricot Glaze. Spread glaze over brownies and let stand until glaze sets, at least 2 hours. Cut in 25 squares.

Apricot Glaze

In a small saucepan over low heat, combine chocolate, jam, butter and vinegar and melt stirring until smooth. Let stand until cool, but pourable.

Sinfully Rich Rocky Roadies

Bittersweet, candylike brownies with an adult-pleasing twist–amaretto liqueur in the frosting!

2 OUNCES UNSWEETENED CHOCOLATE

1/3 CUP SEMISWEET CHOCOLATE CHIPS

1 CUP BUTTER OR MARGARINE

1 CUP ALL-PURPOSE FLOUR

1/3 CUP UNSWEETENED COCOA POWDER

1 CUP GRANULATED SUGAR

1 CUP PACKED DARK BROWN SUGAR

2 EGGS

6 TABLESPOONS COLD WATER

2 TABLESPOONS VANILLA EXTRACT

❖

FROSTING

4 OUNCES UNSWEETENED CHOCOLATE

1 CUP BUTTER OR MARGARINE

1/4 CUP ALMOND-FLAVORED LIQUEUR (OR
   1/4 CUP WATER AND 1 TEASPOON
   ALMOND EXTRACT)

1 TABLESPOON VANILLA EXTRACT

2 CUPS POWDERED SUGAR, SIFTED

1-1/2 CUPS MINIATURE MARSHMALLOWS

1 CUP FINELY CHOPPED WALNUTS,
   (OPTIONAL)

Preheat oven to 350F (175C). Grease a 13" x 9" baking pan. In a small saucepan, melt unsweetened chocolate, semisweet chocolate chips and butter or margarine over low heat, stirring until smooth. Remove from heat and let cool to lukewarm. In a small bowl, sift together flour and cocoa. Set aside. In a large bowl, combine sugars. Whisk eggs, water and vanilla together and add to sugars, stirring until thoroughly blended. Stir in cooled chocolate mixture. Fold in dry ingredients, beating 50 strokes by hand. Spread batter into prepared pan. Bake 20 to 25 minutes, or until a wooden pick inserted in the center comes out slightly moist with crumbs. Set pan on a wire rack and cool. Prepare Frosting. Spread evenly over brownies. Cool completely. Cut in 40 squares.

Frosting

In a large saucepan, melt chocolate, butter or margarine, liqueur and vanilla over low heat, stirring constantly until chocolate is melted. Remove from heat and add powdered sugar, mixing thoroughly. Mixture should be thick, but easily stirred. Fold in marshmallows and nuts, if desired.

Helpful Tip: If frosting is too thick, add boiling water to thin, a tablespoon at a time, until frosting reaches desired consistency.

German Chocolate Fudgies

A classic, coco-nutty topper tops off a rich fudge brownie.

2 OUNCES UNSWEETENED CHOCOLATE

1/3 CUP SEMISWEET CHOCOLATE CHIPS

3/4 CUP BUTTER OR MARGARINE

3/4 CUP ALL-PURPOSE FLOUR

1/2 CUP UNSWEETENED COCOA POWDER

1/4 TEASPOON BAKING SODA

1 CUP GRANULATED SUGAR

1/2 CUP PACKED DARK BROWN SUGAR

1 EGG

1/3 CUP COLD WATER

2 TABLESPOONS VANILLA EXTRACT

❖

FROSTING

1 CUP GRANULATED SUGAR

1/2 CUP BUTTER OR MARGARINE

2/3 CUP MILK

1 TEASPOON VANILLA EXTRACT

3 EGG YOLKS, BEATEN

1-1/2 CUPS SHREDDED COCONUT

1 CUP FINELY CHOPPED PECANS

Preheat oven to 350F (175C). Grease a 9-inch-square baking pan. In a small saucepan, melt unsweetened chocolate, semisweet chocolate chips and butter or margarine over low heat, stirring until smooth. Remove from heat and let cool to lukewarm. In a small bowl, sift together flour, cocoa and baking soda. Set aside. In a large bowl, combine sugars. Whisk egg, water and vanilla together and add to sugars, stirring until thoroughly blended. Stir in cooled chocolate mixture. Fold in flour mixture, beating 50 strokes by hand. Spread batter into prepared pan. Bake 20 to 25 minutes, or until a wooden pick inserted in center comes out slightly moist with crumbs. Set on a wire rack and cool in pan. Prepare Frosting. Spread frosting over brownies, covering completely. Refrigerate until set, at least 1 hour. Cut in 25 squares. Store in refrigerator.

Frosting

In a large heavy saucepan, mix sugar, butter or margarine, milk, vanilla and egg yolks. Cook over medium heat about 12 minutes, stirring occasionally, until thick. Remove from heat. Fold in coconut and pecans. Beat until of spreading consistency. Cool.

Italian Ricotta Cheesecake Brownies

*Mama mia! An Italian cheesecake staple–ricotta cheese (it's low-fat, too!)–in
a melt-in-your mouth brownie that's studded with chocolate chips, raisins and nuts.*

1/2 CUP BUTTER OR MARGARINE,
    SOFTENED
1/2 CUP GRANULATED SUGAR
1/2 CUP PACKED DARK BROWN SUGAR
1 EGG
1 CUP RICOTTA CHEESE
1 TABLESPOON VANILLA EXTRACT
1/4 CUP ANISETTE LIQUEUR (OR
    SUBSTITUTE 1/4 CUP WATER AND 1
    TEASPOON ANISE EXTRACT)
2 CUPS ALL-PURPOSE FLOUR
1/2 CUP UNSWEETENED COCOA POWDER
1/2 TEASPOON BAKING SODA
1 CUP SEMISWEET CHOCOLATE CHIPS
3/4 CUP RAISINS
1/2 CUP CHOPPED WALNUTS (OPTIONAL)

❖

ANISETTE-SPICED FUDGE FROSTING
1/4 CUP BUTTER OR MARGARINE,
    SOFTENED
3/4 CUP GRANULATED SUGAR
1-1/2 OUNCES UNSWEETENED CHOCOLATE
1 CUP SEMISWEET CHOCOLATE CHIPS
1/2 CUP MILK
2 CUPS POWDERED SUGAR
2 TEASPOONS VANILLA EXTRACT
ANISETTE OR WATER

Preheat oven to 375F (190C). Grease a 13" x 9" baking pan. In a large bowl, cream butter or margarine and sugars until light and fluffy. Beat in egg, ricotta cheese and vanilla. Blend in anisette. In a small bowl, sift together flour, cocoa and baking soda. Gradually add dry ingredients to creamed mixture, beating thoroughly. Fold in semisweet chocolate chips, raisins and walnuts, if desired. Spread batter evenly into prepared pan. Bake 20 minutes, or until a wooden pick inserted in center comes out clean. Set on a wire rack and cool in pan. Prepare Anisette-Spiced Fudge Frosting. Frost cooled brownies. Let frosting set before cutting, about 1 hour. Cut in 32 squares.

Anisette-Spiced Fudge Frosting
In a medium saucepan, combine butter or margarine, sugar, semisweet chocolate chips and milk. Bring to a boil, stirring constantly, and cook about 3 minutes. Remove from heat. Blend in powdered sugar and vanilla, beating until creamy. Add 1 to 2 tablespoons anisette (or water) to achieve good spreading consistency.

Fudgy Rum Raisin Brownies

*There's no better companion to a scoop of luscious
vanilla ice cream than these rummy, raisin-filled brownies!*

4 OUNCES UNSWEETENED CHOCOLATE

1 CUP BUTTER OR MARGARINE

1 CUP SUGAR

2 EGGS

1/3 CUP DARK RUM

1 TABLESPOON VANILLA EXTRACT

1 CUP ALL-PURPOSE FLOUR

1/2 CUP RAISINS

Preheat oven to 375F (190C). Grease a 13" x 9" baking pan. In a large saucepan over low heat, melt chocolate and butter or margarine, stirring until smooth. Remove from heat and stir in sugar. Add eggs, one at a time, and stir until batter is shiny. Add rum and vanilla. Gradually add flour and mix until blended. Fold in raisins. Spread batter into prepared baking pan. Bake 30 to 35 minutes or until a wooden pick inserted in center comes out barely moist. Set on a wire rack and cool in pan. Cut in 32 squares.

Variation: Substitute one teaspoon of rum extract and 1/3 cup water for 1/3 cup dark rum.

Mocha Cheesecake Brownies

A sinfully rich brownie that is sure to tantalize the taste buds!

1/2 CUP BUTTER OR MARGARINE
2 OUNCES UNSWEETENED CHOCOLATE
1/4 CUP SEMISWEET CHOCOLATE CHIPS
1 CUP PACKED DARK BROWN SUGAR
1/2 CUP GRANULATED SUGAR
2 TEASPOONS VANILLA EXTRACT
1 EGG
1/3 CUP COFFEE FLAVORED LIQUEUR
3/4 CUP ALL-PURPOSE FLOUR
1/2 CUP UNSWEETENED COCOA POWDER
1/4 TEASPOON BAKING SODA
1/4 TEASPOON BAKING POWDER
1 CUP SEMISWEET CHOCOLATE CHIPS
3/4 CUP SHREDDED COCONUT
1 CUP CHOPPED NUTS (OPTIONAL)

❖

CHEESECAKE TOPPING
8 OUNCES CREAM CHEESE, SOFTENED
1/3 CUP GRANULATED SUGAR
1 EGG
1 TEASPOON VANILLA EXTRACT
3/4 TEASPOON ORANGE EXTRACT (OR 1
   TABLESPOON GRATED ORANGE PEEL)

Preheat oven to 375F (190C). Grease a 9-inch-square baking pan. In a small saucepan over low heat, melt butter or margarine, unsweetened chocolate and semisweet chocolate chips, stirring until smooth. Remove from heat and let cool until lukewarm. In a large bowl, combine sugars. Beat in melted chocolate mixture and vanilla. Whisk egg and coffee flavored liqueur together and add to chocolate mixture, mixing thoroughly. Sift together dry ingredients and add to chocolate mixture, beating 50 strokes until blended. Spread batter into prepared pan and set aside. Prepare Cheesecake Topping. Pour over brownie mixture. Combine chocolate chips, coconut and nuts, if desired, and sprinkle over cheesecake mixture. Bake 25 to 30 minutes or until a wooden pick inserted in center comes out barely moist and Cheesecake Topping is golden and set. Set on a wire rack and cool in pan. Cut in 25 squares. Store in refrigerator.

Cheesecake Topping

Beat cream cheese, sugar, egg, vanilla and orange extract (or orange peel) until thoroughly blended.

Aloha Brownies

A taste of the Hawaiian tropics—it's a perfect summer treat.

3 OUNCES UNSWEETENED CHOCOLATE
1-1/2 CUPS ALL-PURPOSE FLOUR
1/2 TEASPOON BAKING POWDER
1/4 TEASPOON GROUND CINNAMON
1 CUP BUTTER OR MARGARINE, SOFTENED
2 CUPS SUGAR
4 EGGS
1 TEASPOON VANILLA EXTRACT
1/2 TEASPOON COCONUT EXTRACT
1 (15-1/2-OZ.) CAN CRUSHED PINEAPPLE,
   DRAINED
1/2 CUP CHOPPED MACADAMIA NUTS
1/2 CUP SHREDDED COCONUT

Preheat oven to 350F (175C). Grease a 13" x 9" baking pan. In a small saucepan over low heat, melt chocolate. Remove from heat and let cool. In a small bowl, combine flour, baking powder and cinnamon. Set aside. In a large bowl, beat together butter or margarine and sugar until light and fluffy. Add eggs, vanilla and coconut extract and mix well. Gradually add flour mixture and beat until blended and smooth. Measure out 1-1/2 cups of the batter and stir in the pineapple. Set aside. Mix the melted chocolate in remaining batter. Fold in nuts. Spread chocolate batter into prepared pan. Spread pineapple batter over top. Bake 30 minutes. Remove pan from oven and sprinkle coconut over top. Bake an additional 5 to 10 minutes, or until coconut is golden brown and wooden pick inserted in center comes out barely moist. Set on a wire rack and cool in pan. Cut in 24 squares.

The Royal Brownie Torte

An impressive dessert, fit for kings and queens, yet easy enough for a jester to make!

1/2 CUP BUTTER OR MARGARINE
1/2 CUP LIGHT CORN SYRUP
5 OUNCES SEMISWEET CHOCOLATE
3/4 CUP SUGAR
1 TEASPOON VANILLA EXTRACT
3 EGGS
1 CUP ALL-PURPOSE FLOUR
1 CUP CHOPPED PECANS

CHOCOLATE GLAZE
3 OUNCES SEMISWEET CHOCOLATE
2 TEASPOONS BUTTER OR MARGARINE
2 TABLESPOONS LIGHT CORN SYRUP
1 TEASPOON MILK

Preheat oven to 350F (175C). Grease an 8-inch-round cake pan. Line the bottom of the pan with parchment or waxed paper. Grease paper. In a large saucepan over medium heat, bring butter or margarine and corn syrup to a boil, stirring constantly. Add chocolate and stir until melted. Add sugar and vanilla, mixing well. Remove from heat and let cool. When chocolate mixture is cool, beat in eggs, one at a time. Gradually add flour, beating until smooth. Fold in nuts. Spread batter into prepared pan. Bake 30 minutes or until a wooden pick inserted in center comes out barely moist. Set on a wire rack and cool in pan. Prepare Chocolate Glaze. Carefully lift brownie from pan and removed wax paper: place on wire rack with a plate underneath. Pour glaze on top of brownie and spread along sides. The glaze will drip off the sides. Allow glaze to set, about 1 hour, then carefully transfer brownie to a serving plate. Cut in 8 pieces.

Chocolate Glaze

In a small saucepan over low heat, melt chocolate and butter or margarine. Add corn syrup and milk. Stir until smooth. Remove from heat.

Lemon Zinger Brownies

A snappy combination of lemon and chocolate is a zesty, mouth-watering twist on traditional fudge brownies!

8 OUNCES SEMISWEET CHOCOLATE

1/2 CUP BUTTER OR MARGARINE

3 TABLESPOONS ALL-PURPOSE FLOUR

3 TABLESPOONS UNSWEETENED COCOA
   POWDER

1/4 TEASPOON BAKING POWDER

1/4 TEASPOON BAKING SODA

1-1/4 CUPS SUGAR

1 TEASPOON GRATED LEMON PEEL

1 EGG

2 TEASPOONS VANILLA EXTRACT

1/4 CUP LEMON JUICE

❖

LEMON GLAZE

3/4 CUP POWDERED SUGAR

2 TABLESPOONS LEMON JUICE

Preheat oven to 350F (175C). Grease a 9-inch-square baking pan. In a small saucepan over low heat, melt chocolate and butter or margarine, stirring until smooth. Remove from heat and let cool to lukewarm. In a small bowl, sift together flour, cocoa, baking powder and baking soda. Set aside. In a medium bowl, beat together sugar, lemon peel and egg. Add chocolate mixture, vanilla and lemon juice, mixing thoroughly. Add flour mixture and stir until blended and smooth. Spread batter into prepared pan and bake 25 to 30 minutes or until a wooden pick inserted in center comes out barely moist. Set on a wire rack and allow to cool in pan while preparing Lemon Glaze. Drizzle over top of warm brownies. Cool completely before cutting. Cut in 16 to 25 squares.

Lemon Glaze

Combine powdered sugar and lemon juice.

Helpful Hint: If glaze mixture is too thick, add a drop or two more lemon juice.

Crunchy, Crispy, Chip-Filled Brownies

*Rice cereal, nuts, marshmallows, peanut butter and chocolate
and butterscotch chips make for a gooey, fudgy, crunchy surprise!*

3/4 CUP ALL-PURPOSE FLOUR

1/4 TEASPOON BAKING POWDER

2 TABLESPOONS UNSWEETENED COCOA
   POWDER

1/2 CUP BUTTER OR MARGARINE,
   SOFTENED

3/4 CUP SUGAR

2 EGGS

1 TEASPOON VANILLA EXTRACT

1/2 CUP CHOPPED WALNUTS OR PECANS

2 CUPS MINIATURE MARSHMALLOWS

1/2 CUP SEMISWEET CHOCOLATE CHIPS

1 CUP SMOOTH PEANUT BUTTER

1/2 CUP BUTTERSCOTCH CHIPS

1-1/2 CUPS PUFFED RICE CEREAL

Preheat oven to 350F (175C). Grease a 13" x 9" baking pan. In a small bowl, combine flour, baking powder and cocoa. Set aside. In a large bowl, beat together butter or margarine and sugar until light and fluffy. Beat in eggs and vanilla. Gradually add flour mixture until blended and smooth. Fold in nuts. Spread batter into prepared pan and bake 15 minutes. Remove from oven. Sprinkle marshmallows over top of brownies. Bake for 3 minutes. Set on a wire rack and cool in pan. In a small saucepan over low heat, melt chocolate chips and peanut butter, stirring until smooth. Gently fold in butterscotch chips and rice cereal. Spread mixture on top of brownies and allow to cool completely before cutting. Cut in 24 squares.

Variation: For extra crunch, substitute 1 cup crunchy peanut butter and 1-1/2 cups crispy rice cereal for 1 cup smooth peanut butter and 1-1/2 cups puffed rice cereal.

Fudge Brownie Melt-Aways

Melt-in-your-mouth layered buttercream brownie bars—definite party pleasers!

1/2 CUP BUTTER OR MARGARINE

2 OUNCES UNSWEETENED CHOCOLATE

1 EGG

1/4 CUP WATER

1 CUP SUGAR

2 TEASPOONS VANILLA EXTRACT

3/4 CUP ALL-PURPOSE FLOUR

1/3 CUP UNSWEETENED COCOA POWDER

1/4 TEASPOON BAKING POWDER

1/4 TEASPOON BAKING SODA

1 CUP SHREDDED COCONUT

2 OUNCES UNSWEETENED CHOCOLATE

2 TABLESPOONS LIGHT CORN SYRUP

HOT WATER

❖

BUTTERCREAM FROSTING

1/3 CUP BUTTER OR MARGARINE,
  SOFTENED

2 CUPS POWDERED SUGAR

2 TEASPOONS VANILLA EXTRACT

1 TO 2 TABLESPOONS MILK OR CREAM

Preheat oven to 350F (175C). Grease a 9-inch-square baking pan. In a small saucepan, melt butter or margarine and chocolate; set aside. In a medium bowl, whisk egg and water; gradually add sugar, blending thoroughly. Stir in chocolate mixture and vanilla. Sift together flour, cocoa, baking powder and baking soda and stir into chocolate mixture, beating 50 strokes by hand. Fold in coconut. Spread butter or margarine into prepared pan. Bake 20 to 25 minutes, or until a wooden pick inserted in center comes out barely moist with crumbs. Set on a wire rack and cool completely in pan. Prepare Buttercream Frosting and frost cooled brownies. Refrigerate until frosting is firm, 30 to 40 minutes. In a small saucepan, melt chocolate with corn syrup. Add hot water, 1 teaspoon at a time, to achieve desired spreading consistency. Cool slightly and spread over chilled frosting. Chill. Cut in 36 squares. Store in refrigerator.

Buttercream Frosting

In a medium bowl, beat butter or margarine and sugar. Add vanilla and enough milk or cream to make creamy frosting.

Marshmallow Brownies

Miniature marshmallows disappear in the batter to make these fudgy squares absolutely delectable.

4 OUNCES UNSWEETENED CHOCOLATE

1 CUP BUTTER OR MARGARINE

1-1/2 CUPS SUGAR

2 TEASPOONS VANILLA EXTRACT

4 EGGS

1 CUP ALL-PURPOSE FLOUR

2 CUPS MINIATURE MARSHMALLOWS

1 CUP FINELY CHOPPED PECANS

1 TABLESPOON BRANDY OR RUM

POWDERED SUGAR

Preheat oven to 350F (175C). Grease and flour a 13" x 9" baking pan. In a medium saucepan over low heat, melt chocolate and butter or margarine. Remove from heat and stir in sugar, then vanilla. Beat in eggs, one at a time, stirring until blended and smooth. Stir in flour, marshmallows, pecans and liquor. Spread into prepared pan. Bake 25 to 30 minutes, or until a wooden pick inserted in center comes out barely moist with crumbs. Set on a wire rack and cool in pan. Dust lightly with powdered sugar. Cut in 30 squares.

Marbled Brownie Squares

*Light blondie batter is marbled through dark fudge
brownie batter to create these unique, two-tone dessert bars.*

BROWNIE BATTER

2 OUNCES UNSWEETENED CHOCOLATE

1/2 CUP BUTTER OR MARGARINE

1 CUP GRANULATED SUGAR

2 TEASPOONS VANILLA EXTRACT

2 EGGS

1/2 CUP ALL-PURPOSE FLOUR

❖

BLONDIE BATTER

1/3 CUP BUTTER OR MARGARINE

1 CUP PACKED DARK BROWN SUGAR

1 EGG

1 TEASPOON VANILLA EXTRACT

1 CUP ALL-PURPOSE FLOUR

1/2 TEASPOON BAKING POWDER

1/8 TEASPOON BAKING SODA

POWDERED SUGAR

Preheat oven to 350F (175C). Grease a 13" x 9" baking pan. Prepare Brownie Batter; pour into prepared pan and set aside. Prepare Blondie Batter and dollop on top of brownies, gently marbling with a knife. Bake 20 to 25 minutes, or until a wooden pick inserted in center comes out barely moist with crumbs. Set on a wire rack and cool in pan. Dust with powdered sugar. Cut in 30 squares.

Brownie Batter

In a medium saucepan over low heat, melt chocolate and butter or margarine, stirring constantly. Remove from heat and stir in sugar and vanilla. Add eggs, mixing until smooth and satiny. Stir in flour, blending well.

Blondie Batter

In a medium saucepan over medium-low heat, melt butter or margarine. Add brown sugar and allow to cook over medium heat 1 minute. Remove from heat and cool to lukewarm. Add egg and vanilla, mixing until smooth. Sift together flour, baking powder and baking soda and stir into brown sugar mixture blending well.

Chocolate Cream Liqueur Brownies

A traditional brownie spiced with chocolate cream
liqueur makes a delectable addition to all your dessert feasts.

4 OUNCES UNSWEETENED CHOCOLATE

1 CUP BUTTER OR MARGARINE

3 EGGS

1/4 CUP CHOCOLATE CREAM LIQUEUR

1 TABLESPOON VANILLA EXTRACT

2 CUPS SUGAR

1-1/4 CUPS ALL-PURPOSE FLOUR

1 CUP PECANS, COARSELY CHOPPED
    (OPTIONAL)

Preheat oven to 350F (175C). Grease a 13" x 9" baking pan. In a large saucepan over low heat, melt chocolate and butter or margarine, stirring until smooth. Remove from heat and cool to lukewarm. Stir eggs, one at a time, until mixture is shiny. Add chocolate cream liqueur and vanilla. Stir in sugar. Add flour and nuts, if desired, and stir until well mixed. Pour batter evenly into prepared pan. Bake 30 minutes or until a wooden pick inserted in center comes out barely moist. Set on a wire rack and cool in pan. Cut in 30 squares.

Chapter Three

❖

Blondies

❖

Venture beyond the realm of traditional blondies and discover these newfangled taste sensations. Experience a variety of flavors ranging from fresh berry-filled squares to cool and creamy buttermilk treats. One blondie bite and you'll be hooked!

Blueberry Cheesecake Blondies

Blondies have more fun when they're smothered in blueberries! A secret surprise—blueberry jam—is hidden between butterscotch layers, and fresh blueberry cheesecake topping rivals New York's finest!

1 CUP BUTTER OR MARGARINE, SOFTENED

1-1/2 CUPS PACKED DARK BROWN SUGAR

2 EGGS

1 TABLESPOON VANILLA EXTRACT

1/3 CUP BUTTERMILK

2 CUPS ALL-PURPOSE FLOUR

1 TEASPOON BAKING SODA

1 CUP BLUEBERRY JAM

❖

BLUEBERRY CHEESECAKE TOPPING

8 OUNCES CREAM CHEESE, SOFTENED

1/2 CUP GRANULATED SUGAR

1 EGG

1-1/2 TABLESPOONS LEMON JUICE

2 TEASPOONS VANILLA EXTRACT

1 CUP FRESH BLUEBERRIES, WASHED AND
   PAT-DRIED

Preheat oven to 350F (175C). Grease a 13" x 9" baking pan. In a large bowl, cream butter or margarine and brown sugar. Add eggs, vanilla and buttermilk beating until fluffy. Sift flour and baking soda and stir into creamed mixture. Spread half of blondie mixture evenly into prepared pan. Spoon on blueberry jam, spreading gently over the entire layer. Top with remaining blondie mixture, thoroughly covering jam. Prepare Blueberry Cheesecake Topping; spread over top. Bake blondies in center of oven 30 to 35 minutes, or until a wooden pick inserted in center comes out slightly moist with crumbs and topping is golden and set. Set on a wire rack and cool in pan. Store in refrigerator. Cut in 48 squares.

Blueberry Cheesecake Topping

In a medium bowl, beat all ingredients except blueberries until creamy. Gently fold in blueberries.

Cranberry Orange Blondies

*These wintertime wonders are so good you can serve them throughout
the year using canned cranberry sauce or the good, old-fashioned homemade kind!*

1 CUP UNSALTED BUTTER, SOFTENED

1-1/2 CUPS PACKED DARK BROWN SUGAR

1 EGG

2 TEASPOONS VANILLA EXTRACT

1 TEASPOON GRATED ORANGE PEEL

1/3 CUP ORANGE JUICE

2 CUPS ALL-PURPOSE FLOUR

1 TEASPOON BAKING POWDER

1 CUP CHOPPED WALNUTS

❖

CRANBERRY FILLING

2 CUPS WHOLE-BERRY CRANBERRY
    SAUCE, HOMEMADE OR CANNED

2/3 CUP COARSELY CHOPPED WALNUTS

2 TEASPOONS FINELY GRATED ORANGE
    PEEL

3 TABLESPOONS SUGAR

2 TABLESPOONS ALL-PURPOSE FLOUR

❖

CRUMB TOPPING

1 CUP PACKED DARK BROWN SUGAR

1/2 CUP ALL-PURPOSE FLOUR

1/2 CUP BUTTER OR MARGARINE,
    SOFTENED

Preheat oven to 350F (175C). Grease a 13" x 9" baking pan. In a large bowl, cream (by hand or electric mixer) butter and brown sugar. Add egg, vanilla, orange peel and orange juice, beating until fluffy. Sift flour and baking powder and stir into creamed mixture. Spread half of blondie mixture evenly into prepared pan and set aside while preparing Cranberry Filling. Spoon Cranberry Filling over blondie mixture in prepared pan, spreading gently over the entire layer. Top with remaining blondie mixture, thoroughly covering Cranberry Filling. Prepare Crumb Topping and sprinkle evenly over blondies. Bake blondies in the center of the oven 30 to 35 minutes, or until a wooden pick inserted in center comes out slightly moist with crumbs. Set on a wire rack and cool in pan. Cut in 32 squares.

Cranberry Filling

In a small saucepan, combine cranberry sauce, walnuts and orange peel. Stir sugar and flour together and add to cranberry mixture. Bring filling to a boil over medium heat, stirring until thickened, about 5 minutes. Remove from heat and cool to lukewarm.

Crumb Topping

In a small bowl, combine brown sugar and flour until blended. Cut in butter or margarine with a fork or two knives until mixture is crumbly and resembles small peas.

Variation: Fresh Cranberry Filling—In a medium saucepan over medium heat, combine 1 (12-oz.) bag fresh cranberries (finely chopped), 1/2 cup sugar, 2 teaspoons grated orange peel, 2 tablespoons orange juice, 2 tablespoons water and 1/2 cup chopped pecans. Bring to a boil and cook 2 minutes, stirring constantly. Remove from heat and cool slightly. Proceed as directed above.

O' Cherry, O' Cherry O' Blondies

A double dose of chocolate—white in the middle, dark on top—enhances these cherry-filled blondies.

1/3 CUP BUTTER OR MARGARINE

1 CUP WHITE CHOCOLATE CHIPS

1-1/4 CUPS ALL-PURPOSE FLOUR

1/4 TEASPOON BAKING POWDER

1/2 TEASPOON BAKING SODA

1 CUP PACKED DARK BROWN SUGAR

1 TEASPOON VANILLA EXTRACT

2 TABLESPOONS KIRSCH

1 EGG

1/3 CUP SWEETENED CONDENSED MILK

1 CUP CHOPPED FRESH OR FROZEN BING
    CHERRIES

❖

CHOCOLATE CHERRY ICING

2 OUNCES UNSWEETENED CHOCOLATE

2 TABLESPOONS BUTTER OR MARGARINE

2 TABLESPOONS KIRSCH

2 TABLESPOONS CHERRY JAM

1 CUP SIFTED POWDERED SUGAR

Preheat oven to 350F (175C). Grease a 13" x 9" baking pan. In a small saucepan over low heat, melt butter or margarine and white chocolate chips, stirring until smooth. Remove from heat and let cool to lukewarm. Sift flour, baking powder and baking soda into a small bowl. Set aside. Place brown sugar in a large bowl. Add the cooled chocolate mixture, vanilla and kirsch, stirring until blended. Whisk together egg and condensed milk and blend into chocolate mixture. Stir in flour mixture by hand, beating 50 strokes. Fold in cherries. Spread batter into prepared pan. Bake 25 to 30 minutes, or until a wooden pick inserted in center comes out barely moist. Set on a wire rack and cool in pan. Prepare Chocolate Cherry Icing. Drizzle icing over blondies. Cut in 30 squares.

Chocolate Cherry Icing

In a small saucepan over low heat, melt chocolate, butter or margarine, kirsch and jam, stirring until smooth. Remove from heat and add powdered sugar, stirring until blended. Add boiling water, if necessary, to achieve spreading consistency.

Pineapple Cashew Blondies

You'll find this unique blend of pineapple, cashew butter and coconut absolutely irresistible. Cashew butter can be found in most health food and gourmet stores.

1/3 CUP BUTTER OR MARGARINE

1/4 CUP CASHEW BUTTER

1-1/4 CUPS ALL-PURPOSE FLOUR

1/4 TEASPOON BAKING POWDER

1/4 TEASPOON BAKING SODA

1 CUP PACKED DARK BROWN SUGAR

1 TEASPOON VANILLA EXTRACT

1 EGG

1/3 CUP PINEAPPLE JUICE

1 CUP FRESH OR CANNED PINEAPPLE
    CHUNKS, WELL DRAINED

3/4 CUP SHREDDED COCONUT

Preheat oven to 350F (175C). Grease a 13" x 9" baking pan. In a small saucepan over low heat, melt butter or margarine and cashew butter, stirring until smooth. Remove from heat and let cool to lukewarm. Sift flour, baking powder and baking soda into a small bowl. Set aside. Place brown sugar in a large bowl. Add the cooled cashew mixture and vanilla, stirring until blended. Whisk together egg and pineapple juice and blend into cashew mixture. Stir in flour mixture by hand, beating 50 strokes. Fold in pineapple chunks and coconut. Spread batter into prepared pan. Bake 25 to 30 minutes, or until a wooden pick inserted in center comes out barely moist. Set on a wire rack and cool in pan. Cut in 30 squares.

Very Berry Blondies

Three different berries make these the very, berry best!

1/3 CUP BUTTER OR MARGARINE

1 CUP WHITE CHOCOLATE CHIPS

1-1/4 CUPS ALL-PURPOSE FLOUR

1/4 TEASPOON BAKING POWDER

1/2 TEASPOON BAKING SODA

1/2 CUP GRANULATED SUGAR

1/2 CUP PACKED DARK BROWN SUGAR

1 TEASPOON VANILLA EXTRACT

2 TABLESPOONS BERRY-FLAVORED
   LIQUEUR (OR 2 TABLESPOONS WATER
   PLUS 1 TEASPOON BERRY EXTRACT)

1 EGG

1/3 CUP SWEETENED CONDENSED MILK

1/3 CUP EACH: FRESH BLUEBERRIES,
   RASPBERRIES, BLACKBERRIES

❖

BERRY ICING

1/2 CUP BUTTER OR MARGARINE,
   SOFTENED

1/4 CUP BERRY JAM, ANY FLAVOR

3 CUPS POWDERED SUGAR

MILK, AS NEEDED

Preheat oven to 350F (175C). Grease a 13" x 9" baking pan. In a small saucepan over low heat, melt butter or margarine and white chocolate, stirring until smooth. Remove from heat and let cool to lukewarm. Sift flour, baking powder and baking soda into a small bowl. Set aside. Place the sugars in a large bowl. Add the cooled chocolate mixture, vanilla and liqueur, stirring until blended. Whisk together egg and condensed milk and blend into chocolate mixture. Stir in flour mixture by hand, beating 50 strokes. Gently fold in berries. Spread batter into prepared pan. Bake 25 to 30 minutes, or until a wooden pick inserted in center comes out barely moist. Set on a wire rack and cool in pan. Prepare Berry Icing. Spread icing over cooled blondies. Cut in 30 squares. Store in refrigerator.

Berry Icing

In a small bowl, cream butter or margarine, jam and powdered sugar, mixing until smooth. Add milk, 1 teaspoon at a time, to achieve fluffy, spreadable consistency.

White Chocolate Blondies

A basic blondie with a gourmet's touch. This flavorful blend
of white chocolate and orange is a satisfying after-dinner treat.

1/3 CUP BUTTER OR MARGARINE

2 CUPS WHITE CHOCOLATE CHIPS

1-1/4 CUPS ALL-PURPOSE FLOUR

1/4 TEASPOON BAKING POWDER

1/2 TEASPOON BAKING SODA

1/2 CUP GRANULATED SUGAR

1/2 CUP PACKED DARK BROWN SUGAR

1 TABLESPOON VANILLA EXTRACT

1/2 TEASPOON ORANGE EXTRACT (OR 1
   TEASPOON GRATED ORANGE PEEL AND
   1 TEASPOON ORANGE JUICE)

1 EGG

1/3 CUP SWEETENED CONDENSED MILK

1/2 CUP SEMISWEET CHOCOLATE CHIPS

❖

THIN CHOCOLATE ICING

2 OUNCES UNSWEETENED CHOCOLATE

2 TABLESPOONS BUTTER OR MARGARINE

1 TEASPOON VANILLA EXTRACT

1 CUP SIFTED POWDERED SUGAR

2 TABLESPOONS BOILING WATER

Preheat oven to 350F (175C). Grease a 13" x 9" baking pan. In a small saucepan over low heat, melt butter or margarine and 1 cup of the white chocolate chips, stirring until smooth. Remove from heat and let cool to lukewarm. Sift flour, baking powder and baking soda into a small bowl. Set aside. Place sugars in a large bowl. Add the cooled chocolate mixture, vanilla and orange extract, stirring until well blended. Whisk together egg and condensed milk and blend into chocolate mixture. Stir in flour mixture by hand, beating 50 strokes. Fold in the remaining white chocolate chips and semisweet chocolate chips. Spread batter into prepared pan. Bake 25 to 30 minutes, or until a wooden pick inserted in center comes out barely moist. Set on a wire rack and cool in pan. Prepare Thin Chocolate Icing. Drizzle icing over blondies and refrigerate until set, at least one hour, before cutting. Cut in 30 squares.

Thin Chocolate Icing

In a small saucepan over low heat, melt chocolate and butter or margarine, stirring until smooth. Remove from heat and add vanilla and powdered sugar, stirring until blended. Return to heat and add boiling water, stirring until mixture is smooth and of good spreading consistency.

Traditional Butterscotch Blondies

Here's the real thing–packed with butter, brown sugar and vanilla–it's true blondie heaven.

1/2 CUP BUTTER OR MARGARINE,
  SOFTENED
2 CUPS PACKED DARK BROWN SUGAR
1 TABLESPOON VANILLA EXTRACT
2 EGGS
1 CUP ALL-PURPOSE FLOUR
1 TEASPOON BAKING POWDER
1 CUP BUTTERSCOTCH CHIPS

Preheat oven to 350F (175C). Grease a 13" x 9" baking pan. In a large bowl, cream butter or margarine and brown sugar until light and fluffy. Add vanilla and eggs, beating until blended. Sift together flour and baking powder, add to creamed mixture, beating well. Fold in butterscotch chips. Spread batter evenly into prepared pan. Bake 30 to 35 minutes, or until a wooden pick inserted in center comes out barely moist. Set on a wire rack and cool in pan. Cut in 30 squares.

Blonde Dates

You'll never have a lonely Saturday night again because you can always count on a blonde date!

1/2 CUP FINELY CHOPPED DATES

2 TABLESPOONS ORANGE LIQUEUR

1 TABLESPOON FRESH ORANGE JUICE

1 TABLESPOON GRATED ORANGE PEEL

1 TEASPOON FRESH LEMON JUICE

1 TEASPOON GRATED LEMON PEEL

1 TEASPOON VANILLA EXTRACT

2 TABLESPOONS UNSALTED BUTTER OR
    MARGARINE

3 OUNCES CREAM CHEESE

1 CUP WHITE CHOCOLATE CHIPS OR 8
    OUNCES FINELY CHOPPED WHITE
    CHOCOLATE BAR

2 EGGS

2/3 CUP SUGAR

1 CUP ALL-PURPOSE FLOUR

❖

ORANGE GLAZE

2/3 CUP POWDERED SUGAR

1 TABLESPOON ORANGE-FLAVORED
    LIQUEUR

2 TEASPOONS FRESH ORANGE JUICE

Preheat oven to 350F (175C). Grease a 9-inch-square baking pan. In a medium bowl, combine dates, orange liqueur, orange juice, orange peel, lemon juice, lemon peel and vanilla, set aside. In a small saucepan over low heat, melt butter or margarine and cream cheese, stirring constantly. Remove from heat and fold in 1/2 cup of white chocolate chips. Let stand 5 minutes. Stir gently to combine, then set aside to cool. In a large bowl, whisk eggs and sugar until thickened, about 1 minute. Add cream cheese mixture, stirring well. Fold in date mixture and remaining 1/2 cup white chocolate chips. Fold in flour. Spread batter evenly into prepared pan. Bake 30 to 35 minutes, or until a wooden pick inserted in center comes out barely moist. Set on a wire rack and cool in pan. Prepare Orange Glaze. Spread glaze evenly over blondies. Let stand until glaze sets, about 30 minutes. Cut in 20 squares.

Orange Glaze

Mix all ingredients in a small bowl.

Georgia Peachies

One bite and these will forever be on your mind.

CHOCOLATE BATTER

1/3 CUP BUTTER OR MARGARINE

1 CUP PACKED DARK BROWN SUGAR

1 EGG

1 TEASPOON VANILLA EXTRACT

1 TABLESPOON PEACH BRANDY

1/4 CUP WATER

3/4 CUP ALL-PURPOSE FLOUR

1/2 CUP UNSWEETENED COCOA POWDER

1/2 TEASPOON BAKING SODA

1/2 CUP CHOPPED WALNUTS (OPTIONAL)

❖

PEACH BATTER

2 TABLESPOONS BUTTER OR MARGARINE,
   SOFTENED

3 OUNCES CREAM CHEESE, SOFTENED

1/4 CUP BROWN SUGAR

1 EGG

6 TABLESPOONS ALL-PURPOSE FLOUR

1 TEASPOON VANILLA EXTRACT

1 TABLESPOON PEACH BRANDY

1/2 CUP PUREED FRESH PEACHES
   (PEELED)

❖

PEACH GLAZE

1 CUP SIFTED POWDERED SUGAR

1 MEDIUM PEACH, PEELED AND PUREED

1 TEASPOON PEACH BRANDY

Preheat oven to 350F (175C). Grease a 13" x 9" baking pan. Prepare Chocolate Batter and Peach Batter. Spread 1/2 of Chocolate Batter into prepared pan. Spread Peach Batter on top, covering Chocolate Batter completely. Dollop remaining Chocolate Batter on top, and slightly swirl with knife to marble. Bake 35 to 40 minutes, or until a wooden pick inserted in center comes out clean. Set on a wire rack and cool in pan. Prepare Peach Glaze. Drizzle glaze over blondies. Let stand until glaze sets, about 30 minutes, before cutting. Cut in 32 squares.

Chocolate Batter

In a large saucepan over low heat, melt butter or margarine. Remove from heat and stir in brown sugar. Beat in egg, vanilla, peach brandy and water. Sift together flour, cocoa and baking soda and add to butter mixture, mixing well. Fold in walnuts, if desired.

Peach Batter

In a small bowl, beat together butter or margarine and cream cheese until fluffy. Beat in sugar, egg and flour. Add vanilla, peach brandy and pureed peaches, stirring until blended and smooth.

Peach Glaze

In a small bowl, combine all ingredients, blending until smooth.

Lemon Blondies with Raspberry Glacé Icing

A marriage of two great flavors–lemon and raspberry–will tickle fruit lovers' fancy.

2 CUPS VANILLA WAFER CRUMBS, LIGHTLY
    PACKED
1 (14-OZ.) CAN SWEETENED CONDENSED
    MILK
2 TEASPOONS GRATED LEMON PEEL
1 TEASPOON FRESH LEMON JUICE
3 TABLESPOONS POPPY SEEDS
3/4 CUP FINELY CHOPPED WALNUTS
    (OPTIONAL)

❖

RASPBERRY GLACÉ ICING
2 CUPS POWDERED SUGAR
1 TEASPOON BUTTER OR MARGARINE,
    SOFTENED
1 TO 2 TEASPOONS RASPBERRY LIQUEUR
1/2 CUP FRESH RASPBERRIES
ABOUT 1-1/2 TABLESPOONS HOT WATER

Preheat oven to 350F (175C). Grease a 9-inch-square baking pan. In a medium bowl, combine wafer crumbs, condensed milk, lemon peel and lemon juice, mix until well blended. Fold in poppy seeds and walnuts, if desired. Spread batter evenly into prepared pan. Bake 25 to 30 minutes, or until a wooden pick inserted in center comes out clean. Set on a wire rack and cool in pan. Prepare Raspberry Glacé Icing. Spread onto completely cooled blondies. Let stand until icing sets, about 30 minutes, before cutting. Cut in 20 squares.

Raspberry Glacé Icing

Sift powdered sugar into a small bowl; add butter or margarine, raspberry liqueur and raspberries. Stir in hot water, 1 teaspoon at a time, until mixture is of spreading consistency. You may not need all the water.

Classic Buttercup Blondies

Cool and creamy buttermilk adds a new flavor dimension to a classic blondie.

1-1/4 CUPS ALL-PURPOSE FLOUR

1 TEASPOON BAKING POWDER

2/3 CUP UNSALTED BUTTER OR
   MARGARINE, SOFTENED

1/3 CUP GRANULATED SUGAR

3/4 CUP PACKED DARK BROWN SUGAR

1 EGG

2 TEASPOONS VANILLA EXTRACT

1/4 CUP BUTTERMILK

1 CUP CHOPPED WALNUTS OR PECANS
   (OPTIONAL)

❖

BUTTERCUP FROSTING

1/2 CUP UNSALTED BUTTER OR
   MARGARINE

1/4 CUP BUTTERMILK

1 TEASPOON VANILLA EXTRACT

1 TEASPOON ALMOND EXTRACT

1 TEASPOON LEMON EXTRACT

3 CUPS POWDERED SUGAR

Preheat oven to 350F (175C). Grease a 9-inch-square baking pan. In a small bowl, combine flour and baking powder. In a large bowl, cream butter or margarine and sugars until light and fluffy. Add egg and vanilla, beating well. Blend in buttermilk. Stir in flour mixture just to mix. Fold in nuts, if desired. Spread batter evenly into prepared pan. Bake 25 to 30 minutes, or until a wooden pick inserted in center comes out slightly moist. Set on a wire rack and cool in pan. Prepare Buttercup Frosting. Frost cooled blondies, cover and refrigerate overnight before cutting. Cut in 20 squares. Store in refrigerator.

Buttercup Frosting

In a medium saucepan over low heat, melt butter or margarine. Add buttermilk, vanilla, almond and lemon extracts and blend until smooth. Bring to a boil, stirring constantly, and boil 1 minute. Remove from heat and cool slightly. Place powdered sugar in a large bowl. Gradually beat in buttermilk mixture until thick and smooth; do not over beat.

Variation: Replace nuts in blondie batter with 1 cup semisweet chocolate chips.

Fancy Fruit-Nut Blondies

A nutty combination of black currant jam and pecans that's sure to be the toast of every party.

1/2 CUP BUTTER OR MARGARINE,
   SOFTENED
1/2 CUP SIFTED POWDERED SUGAR
2 EGG YOLKS
1 CUP ALL-PURPOSE FLOUR
3/4 CUP BLACK CURRANT JAM

❖

MERINGUE-PECAN TOPPING
2 EGG WHITES
1/2 CUP GRANULATED SUGAR
1/4 TEASPOON GROUND CINNAMON
1 CUP FINELY CHOPPED PECANS

Preheat oven to 350F (175C). Grease a 13" x 9" baking pan. In a medium bowl, mix butter or margarine, powdered sugar and egg yolks. Stir in flour. Press into prepared pan, using your hand to flatten evenly over bottom. Bake 10 minutes. Prepare Meringue-Pecan Topping. Spread jam over crust, then spoon on Meringue-Pecan Topping. Bake 20 minutes more, or until topping is golden brown. Set on a wire rack and cool in pan. Cut in 30 bars.

Meringue-Pecan Topping

Beat egg whites until frothy. Gradually add sugar and cinnamon; beat until stiff and glossy. Fold in pecans.

Oatmeal Blondies

Wholesome, chocolate-chip-filled oat blondies topped with a tangy orange syrup.

1/2 CUP BUTTER OR MARGARINE,
    SOFTENED
2/3 CUP PACKED DARK BROWN SUGAR
2 TEASPOONS VANILLA EXTRACT
1 EGG
1/2 CUP BUTTERMILK
1 CUP ALL-PURPOSE FLOUR
1/4 TEASPOON BAKING SODA
1-1/4 CUPS ROLLED OATS
1-1/2 CUPS SEMISWEET CHOCOLATE CHIPS
1/2 CUP GRANULATED SUGAR
3 TABLESPOONS ORANGE JUICE
1 TEASPOON GRATED ORANGE PEEL

Preheat oven to 350F (175C). Grease a 9-inch-square baking pan. In a medium bowl, cream butter or margarine, brown sugar and vanilla until light and fluffy. Add egg, blending thoroughly. Stir in buttermilk. Sift together flour and baking soda and add to buttermilk mixture, blending well. Stir in oats and chocolate chips. Spread into prepared pan. Bake 25 to 30 minutes, or until a wooden pick inserted in center comes out barely moist with crumbs. Just before blondies are done, mix sugar and orange juice in a small saucepan. Bring to a boil over medium heat. Remove from heat; stir in peel. Pour hot syrup over blondies. Set on a wire rack and cool in pan. Cut in 25 bars.

Pecan-Praline Blondies

Crunchy, heavenly blondies filled with brown sugar, pecan praline and luscious white chocolate.

BLONDIES

3 OUNCES WHITE CHOCOLATE, COARSELY
  CHOPPED
1/4 CUP BUTTER OR MARGARINE,
  SOFTENED
1/2 CUP PACKED LIGHT BROWN SUGAR
1 EGG
1 TEASPOON VANILLA EXTRACT
1 TABLESPOON BRANDY OR RUM
1 CUP ALL-PURPOSE FLOUR
2 OUNCES WHITE CHOCOLATE, GRATED

❖

PECAN PRALINE

1/3 CUP PACKED DARK BROWN SUGAR
2 TABLESPOONS BRANDY OR RUM
3/4 CUP COARSELY CHOPPED UNSALTED
  PECANS

Blondies

Preheat oven to 350F (175C). Line an 8-inch-square baking pan with foil so that the foil extends 2 inches beyond the edges of the pan. Grease the bottom and sides of the foiled pan. In a small saucepan over low heat, melt white chocolate, stirring constantly. Remove from heat and cool about 5 minutes. Add butter or margarine, 1 tablespoon at a time, whisking until smooth after each addition. Set aside. In a large bowl, beat brown sugar and egg for 2 minutes on high speed of electric mixer. Beat in vanilla and brandy or rum. Fold in the white chocolate mixture. Stir in flour and 1/3 cup of Pecan Praline. Spread batter into prepared pan. Bake 18 minutes. Sprinkle blondies with remaining Pecan Praline and bake 6 to 8 minutes more, or until a wooden pick inserted in center comes out barely moist with crumbs. Sprinkle hot blondies with grated white chocolate. Set on a wire rack and cool in pan at least 1 hour before cutting. Lift blondies from the pan using the foil handles. Cut in 16 squares, carefully removing from foil.

Pecan Praline

Lightly grease a small baking sheet. In a small, heavy saucepan, combine brown sugar and brandy or rum. Cook over medium heat, stirring constantly, until the sugar dissolves. Increase the heat to high and bring the syrup to a boil. Cook without stirring, 4 minutes or until the syrup caramelizes. Remove from heat immediately and add pecans, stirring to coat with syrup. Quickly turn onto greased baking sheet. Cool 20 minutes, or until hardened. Finely chop praline with a sharp knife. Set aside.

Oatmeal Raisin Bars

Chewy, good-for-you bar cookies filled with oatmeal, raisins and nuts.

1 CUP DARK RAISINS

1 CUP GOLDEN RAISINS

1 (14-OZ.) CAN SWEETENED CONDENSED
   MILK

1 TABLESPOON GRATED LEMON PEEL

1 TABLESPOON LEMON JUICE

1 CUP BUTTER OR MARGARINE, SOFTENED

1-1/4 CUPS PACKED DARK BROWN SUGAR

2 TEASPOONS VANILLA EXTRACT

2-1/2 CUPS ROLLED OATS

1 CUP ALL-PURPOSE FLOUR

1/2 TEASPOON BAKING SODA

1 CUP CHOPPED WALNUTS OR PECANS

Preheat oven to 375F (190C). Grease a 13" x 9" baking pan. In a medium saucepan, combine raisins, condensed milk, lemon peel and lemon juice. Cook over medium heat, stirring constantly, just until mixture begins to bubble. Remove from heat and allow to cool. In a large bowl, beat butter or margarine, brown sugar and vanilla until fluffy. Add remaining ingredients, stirring until well blended and crumbly. Reserve 2 cups of oat mixture for topping; press remaining mixture into prepared pan. Spread raisin filling over oat mixture in pan; crumble remaining oat mixture over top. Bake 25 to 30 minutes, or until golden brown. Set on a wire rack and cool in pan. Cut in 35 bars.

Butterscotch Meringue Blondies

Brown sugar meringue tops off these chewy butterscotch blondies.

1-3/4 CUPS ALL-PURPOSE FLOUR

1 TEASPOON BAKING POWDER

1/2 CUP BUTTER OR MARGARINE,
  SOFTENED

1-1/2 CUPS PACKED DARK BROWN SUGAR

2 EGGS

2 TEASPOONS VANILLA EXTRACT

1 CUP CHOPPED WALNUTS (OPTIONAL)

Preheat oven to 350F (175C). Grease a 13" x 9" baking pan. Sift together flour and baking powder; set aside. In a large bowl, cream butter or margarine and 1 cup brown sugar until light and fluffy. Add 1 whole egg and 1 egg yolk (reserve egg white) to sugar mixture, beating well. Add 1-1/2 teaspoons vanilla. Stir in flour mixture, blending thoroughly. Stir in walnuts, if desired. Spread mixture into prepared pan. Set aside. In a small bowl, beat egg white until stiff but not dry. Beat in remaining sugar and vanilla. Spread thinly over blondie batter. Bake 30 minutes, or until golden brown. Set on a wire rack and cool in pan. Cut in 30 bars.

Chapter Four

❖

Bar
Cookies

❖

A piece of cake to bake, bar cookies taste
great! From sunup to sundown, you'll
find a recipe to satisfy your sweet tooth
any time of day. From CJ's Cereal
Crunches to Midnight Munchies, here's
a chapter full of tasty treats.

Coffee Breakers

It's coffee time! And what better companion than these quick and easy coffee-kissed bars.

2 CUPS VANILLA WAFER CRUMBS, LIGHTLY
    PACKED
1 (14-OZ.) CAN SWEETENED CONDENSED
    MILK
1 TABLESPOON INSTANT COFFEE POWDER,
    DISSOLVED IN A LITTLE BOILING WATER
1 TEASPOON VANILLA EXTRACT
1/2 TEASPOON ALMOND EXTRACT
1/3 CUP MILK CHOCOLATE CHIPS
1/3 CUP SEMISWEET CHOCOLATE CHIPS

Preheat oven to 350F (175C). Grease a 9-inch-square baking pan. In a medium bowl, combine wafer crumbs, condensed milk, dissolved coffee powder, vanilla and almond extract, mixing well. Fold in milk chocolate and semisweet chocolate chips. Spread batter evenly into prepared pan. Bake 25 to 30 minutes, or until a wooden pick inserted in center comes out clean. Set on a wire rack and cool in pan. Cut in 16 squares.

Pecan-Praline Chocolate Bars

Excellent—is the word that best describes these incredibly delectable chocolate-pecan, orange-flavored bars!

BROWN SUGAR CRUST

1 CUP ALL-PURPOSE FLOUR

1/4 CUP PACKED DARK BROWN SUGAR

1/2 CUP BUTTER OR MARGARINE,
   SOFTENED

2 TEASPOONS VANILLA EXTRACT

1 CUP SEMISWEET CHOCOLATE CHIPS

❖

PECAN FILLING

1/2 CUP BUTTER OR MARGARINE, MELTED

1-1/2 CUPS PACKED DARK BROWN SUGAR

1 EGG

2 TABLESPOONS FRESH ORANGE JUICE

1 TEASPOON GRATED ORANGE PEEL

2 TEASPOONS VANILLA EXTRACT

1-1/4 CUPS ALL-PURPOSE FLOUR

1 TEASPOON BAKING POWDER

1-1/2 CUPS CHOPPED PECANS

❖

THIN CHOCOLATE COATING

2 OUNCES UNSWEETENED CHOCOLATE

2 TABLESPOONS BUTTER OR MARGARINE

1 TEASPOON VANILLA EXTRACT

1 CUP SIFTED POWDERED SUGAR

2 TABLESPOONS BOILING WATER

Preheat oven to 350F (175C). Lightly grease a 13" x 9" baking pan. Prepare Brown Sugar Crust. Bake 13 to 15 minutes, or until edges are golden. While crust is baking, prepare Pecan Filling. Set aside. Remove crust from oven; immediately sprinkle with chocolate chips. Bake 2 to 3 minutes or until chocolate melts. Remove from oven and, with a knife, spread melted chocolate evenly over baked crust. Spread Pecan Filling over melted chocolate. Bake 20 to 25 minutes, or until golden. Set on a wire rack and cool in pan. Prepare Thin Chocolate Coating. Drizzle coating over pecan bars. Refrigerate until icing is set, at least one hour before cutting. Cut in 48 squares.

Brown Sugar Crust

In a medium bowl, combine flour, brown sugar and butter or margarine; blend until crumbly. Add vanilla and mix until dough sticks together. Press evenly into prepared pan.

Pecan Filling

In a large bowl, combine melted butter or margarine and brown sugar. Add egg, orange juice, orange peel and vanilla, beating well. Mix in flour and baking powder, stirring until blended. Stir in chopped pecans.

Thin Chocolate Coating

In a small saucepan over low heat, melt chocolate and butter or margarine, stirring until smooth. Remove from heat and add vanilla and powdered sugar, stirring until blended. Return to heat and add boiling water, stirring until mixture is smooth and of good spreading consistency.

Chewy Chocolate Chip Bars

An extra-rich, easy-to-make bar cookie version of everyone's favorite cookie.

1 CUP BUTTER OR MARGARINE, SOFTENED

1 CUP PACKED DARK BROWN SUGAR

2 TEASPOONS VANILLA EXTRACT

2 CUPS ALL-PURPOSE FLOUR

1-1/2 CUPS SEMISWEET CHOCOLATE CHIPS

1 CUP FINELY CHOPPED WALNUTS
   (OPTIONAL)

Preheat oven to 350F (175C). Grease a 13" x 9" baking pan. In a large bowl, cream butter or margarine and sugar until light and fluffy. Add vanilla, mixing well. Add flour to sugar mixture, stirring until blended. Stir in chocolate chips and walnuts, if desired. Press dough evenly into prepared pan. Bake 15 to 18 minutes, or until a wooden pick inserted in center comes out moist. Set on a wire rack and cool in pan. Cut in 42 bars.

Health-Nut Hunks

All sorts of good-for-you grains, fruits and nuts go into these chewy, healthful bars.

1/2 CUP BUTTER OR MARGARINE

1/4 CUP PEANUT BUTTER

1/2 CUP HONEY

1 CUP PACKED DARK BROWN SUGAR

2 CUPS ROLLED OATS

1 CUP PUFFED RICE CEREAL

1 CUP UNPROCESSED BRAN FLAKES

1/2 CUP BRAN CEREAL

1/2 CUP WHEAT GERM

1/2 CUP SHREDDED COCONUT

1/4 CUP SESAME SEEDS

1/2 CUP SUNFLOWER KERNELS

1/2 CUP DRIED APRICOTS, CHOPPED

1/2 CUP DATES, CHOPPED

1/2 CUP GOLDEN RAISINS

Preheat oven to 350F (175C). Grease a 13" x 9" baking pan. In a large skillet over low heat, melt together butter or margarine, peanut butter, honey and brown sugar, stirring occasionally to blend. Add remaining ingredients, stirring until blended. Cook over low heat 10 minutes, or until golden brown, stirring constantly to avoid burning. Spread into prepared pan. Press mixture lightly. Cool. Cut in 35 bars.

Peanut Butter Toffee Bars

Chewy, candylike brown sugar bars topped with peanut butter and chocolate are sure to be a hit.

1 CUP BUTTER OR MARGARINE, SOFTENED
1 CUP PACKED DARK BROWN SUGAR
1 EGG YOLK
1 TABLESPOON VANILLA EXTRACT
2 CUPS ALL-PURPOSE FLOUR

❖

PEANUT BUTTER TOPPING
2 CUPS SEMISWEET CHOCOLATE CHIPS
1/2 CUP PEANUT BUTTER

Preheat oven to 350F (175C). Grease a 13" x 9" baking pan. In a large bowl, cream butter or margarine, brown sugar, egg yolk and vanilla until light and fluffy. Add flour to sugar mixture, stirring until blended. Press dough evenly in prepared pan. Bake 15 to 18 minutes or until a wooden pick inserted in center comes out slightly moist. Set on a wire rack and cool in pan. Meanwhile, prepare Peanut Butter Topping. Spread topping over bars. Cool completely before cutting. Cut in 48 bars.

Peanut Butter Topping
In a medium saucepan over low heat, melt together chocolate chips and peanut butter, stirring until smooth.

Variation: Melt chocolate chips with 3/4 cup raspberry, cherry or blueberry jam, stirring until blended. Add boiling water as needed to achieve desired spreading consistency.

Caramel Apple Bars

Applesauce and raisins nestled between nutritious oat layers and finished off with creamy butterscotch topping–these chewy treats rival the best county fair caramel apples!

2/3 CUP BUTTER OR MARGARINE,
   SOFTENED
3/4 CUP PACKED DARK BROWN SUGAR
2 TEASPOONS VANILLA EXTRACT
1-1/2 CUPS ALL-PURPOSE FLOUR
1/2 TEASPOON BAKING SODA
1-1/2 TEASPOONS GROUND CINNAMON
1-3/4 CUPS ROLLED OATS
1-1/4 CUPS APPLESAUCE
1 CUP RAISINS
3/4 CUP CHOPPED WALNUTS (OPTIONAL)
1/2 CUP PURCHASED BUTTERSCOTCH ICE
   CREAM TOPPING

Preheat oven to 350F (175C). Grease a 13" x 9" baking pan. In a large bowl, cream butter or margarine, brown sugar and vanilla until light and fluffy. Add flour, baking soda and cinnamon, beating until blended. Stir in oats. Mixture will be crumbly. Press half of oat mixture evenly into prepared pan. In a medium bowl, mix applesauce, raisins and nuts, if desired. Spread evenly over oat mixture. Sprinkle remaining oat mixture over applesauce mixture, pressing in gently. Drizzle butterscotch topping over applesauce-oat mixture. Bake 25 to 30 minutes, or until golden brown. Set on a wire rack and cool in pan. Cut in 48 bars. Store in refrigerator.

Variation: Use golden raisins, chopped pitted dates, apricots or figs as fruity additions.

CJ's Cereal Crunches

The cereal provides the crunch and the coconut the chew in these delicious breakfast treats. Try adding raisins or chocolate chips for a change of pace.

2/3 CUP BUTTER OR MARGARINE

1 CUP WHEAT, OAT OR BRAN CEREAL

1-1/2 CUPS PACKED DARK BROWN SUGAR

2 EGGS

2 TEASPOONS VANILLA EXTRACT

1-1/2 CUPS ALL-PURPOSE FLOUR

1 TEASPOON BAKING POWDER

1/4 TEASPOON BAKING SODA

1-1/2 CUPS FLAKED OR SHREDDED
    COCONUT

Preheat oven to 350F (175C). Grease a 13" x 9" baking pan. In a medium saucepan, melt butter or margarine. Add cereal and cook 2 minutes, stirring constantly. Remove from heat. Stir in brown sugar, mixing thoroughly. Stir in eggs and vanilla until blended. Add flour, baking powder and baking soda to sugar mixture, stirring until blended. Fold in coconut. Spread evenly into prepared pan. Bake 22 to 25 minutes, or until golden brown. Set on a wire rack and cool in pan. Cut in 48 bars while still slightly warm.

Variation: Add 1 cup dark or light raisins and/or 1 cup semisweet chocolate chips with coconut.

Honeyed Carrot Cake Bars

*Cool and dreamy cream cheese frosting tops off these moist
and nutritious carrot bars–they're sure to please carrot cake lovers!*

1/3 CUP VEGETABLE OIL

1/3 CUP HONEY

1/3 CUP PACKED DARK BROWN SUGAR

2 EGGS

2 TEASPOONS VANILLA EXTRACT

1 CUP WHOLE-WHEAT FLOUR

1 TEASPOON BAKING POWDER

1 TEASPOON BAKING SODA

3 TABLESPOONS BUTTERMILK

1/2 CUP WELL-DRAINED CRUSHED,
   UNSWEETENED PINEAPPLE

1 CUP FINELY SHREDDED RAW CARROTS

1/2 CUP CHOPPED WALNUTS

1/3 CUP DARK RAISINS

1/3 CUP GOLDEN RAISINS

❖

CREAM CHEESE FROSTING

3 OUNCES CREAM CHEESE, SOFTENED

1/4 CUP BUTTER OR MARGARINE,
   SOFTENED

1-1/2 CUPS POWDERED SUGAR

1 TEASPOON VANILLA EXTRACT

1 TEASPOON GRATED ORANGE PEEL

BUTTERMILK, AS NEEDED

Preheat oven to 350F (175C). Grease a 13" x 9" baking pan. In a large bowl, combine oil, honey, brown sugar, eggs and vanilla. Add flour, baking powder and baking soda to brown sugar mixture, stirring until blended. Stir in buttermilk, pineapple, carrots, walnuts and raisins, mixing thoroughly. Pour into prepared pan. Bake 25 to 30 minutes, or until a wooden pick inserted in center comes out slightly moist with crumbs. Set on a wire rack and cool in pan. Meanwhile, prepare Cream Cheese Frosting. Spread frosting over cooled bars. Cut in 36 bars. Store in refrigerator.

Cream Cheese Frosting

In a medium bowl, mix cream cheese, butter or margarine and powdered sugar until light and fluffy. Add vanilla and orange peel, blending thoroughly. Add buttermilk, a tablespoon at a time, to achieve desired spreading consistency.

Remarkable Raspberry Meringues

If you thought lemon was the only meringue companion…
think again! Raspberry jam paired with nutty meringue is sure to please your palate.

2-1/2 CUPS ALL-PURPOSE FLOUR

6 TABLESPOONS GRANULATED SUGAR

1 CUP BUTTER OR MARGARINE, SOFTENED

5 EGGS, SEPARATED

1 TABLESPOON VANILLA EXTRACT

3-1/2 CUPS RASPBERRY JAM

POWDERED SUGAR

❖

MERINGUE TOPPING

1 CUP GRANULATED SUGAR

2 CUPS FINELY CHOPPED WALNUTS

Preheat oven to 350F (175C). Grease a 13" x 9" baking pan. In a medium bowl, mix together flour and sugar. With a pastry blender, or using two knives, cut butter into flour mixture until crumbly. Add egg yolks and vanilla and mix until well blended. Press mixture into prepared pan. Bake 10 minutes, or until barely browned. Cool 15 minutes. Spread raspberry jam over cooled crust and set aside while preparing Meringue Topping. Spread Meringue Topping evenly over crust. Bake 30 to 35 minutes until lightly browned. Cool completely and dust with powdered sugar. Cut in 32 squares.

Meringue Topping

In a medium bowl, beat egg whites, gradually adding sugar until soft peaks form. Fold in walnuts.

Laura's #1 Lunch-Box Treats

A piece of cake to bake, you're sure to get many requests for these sweet and chewy delights.

1/2 CUP BUTTER OR MARGARINE

1 CUP GRAHAM CRACKER CRUMBS

1 CUP FLAKED OR SHREDDED COCONUT

1 CUP WALNUTS, CHOPPED

1 CUP CHOCOLATE CHIPS

1 (14-OZ.) CAN SWEETENED CONDENSED
    MILK

Preheat oven to 350F (175C). Place butter or margarine in a 10" x 7" or 9-inch-square baking pan. Melt in oven. Remove pan from oven and stir graham cracker crumbs, pressing gently with the back of a fork to form a crust. Then sprinkle with nuts and chocolate chips. Sprinkle coconut evenly over top. Drizzle condensed milk evenly over coconut. Bake 25 to 30 minutes, or until wooden pick inserted in center comes out moist. Set on a wire rack and cool completely before cutting in squares.

Variation: Substitute butterscotch chips for chocolate chips and pecans for walnuts.

Butterscotch Shortbread

Traditional shortbread prepared in a non-traditional way. These bar cookies will melt in your mouth.

1 CUP BUTTER (MARGARINE NOT
   RECOMMENDED), SOFTENED
1/2 CUP SUPERFINE SUGAR
2 CUPS SIFTED ALL-PURPOSE FLOUR
CANDIED CHERRIES FOR DECORATION, IF
   DESIRED

Preheat oven to 300F (165C). Grease a 9-inch-square baking pan. Cream butter and sugar together until smooth. Add flour and knead until ball forms. Press dough evenly into bottom of prepared pan. With a knife, cut 16 squares, cutting only halfway through dough. Bake 25 minutes, or until light brown. Set on a wire rack and cool 30 minutes before completing cutting.

Oh My Stars! Orange Bars

These delicate squares of orange cookie topped with rich chocolate are perfect served with tea.

1 CUP BUTTER OR MARGARINE, SOFTENED

3/4 CUP SUGAR

1 EGG

1 TEASPOON MILK

1 TEASPOON ORANGE EXTRACT

1 TEASPOON VANILLA EXTRACT

1 TABLESPOON GRATED ORANGE PEEL

2/3 CUP ALL-PURPOSE FLOUR

1/2 TEASPOON BAKING POWDER

1 CUP SHREDDED COCONUT

1 CUP SEMISWEET CHOCOLATE CHIPS,
    MELTED

Preheat oven to 350F (175C). Line an 8-inch-square baking pan with waxed paper; grease paper. In a medium bowl, beat together butter or margarine, sugar, egg, milk, orange extract, vanilla extract and orange peel until light and fluffy. Add flour and baking powder and beat until well blended. Stir in coconut. Spread batter evenly into prepared pan. Bake 30 minutes, or until lightly browned. Immediately, spread melted semisweet chocolate chips evenly over hot bars. Set on a wire rack and cool in pan. Cut in 16 bars.

Tantalizing Toffee Treats

A mouth-watering candylike cookie.

1 CUP BUTTER OR MARGARINE, SOFTENED

1 CUP PACKED DARK BROWN SUGAR

1 EGG YOLK

1 TEASPOON VANILLA EXTRACT

2 CUPS ALL-PURPOSE FLOUR

1 CUP SEMISWEET CHOCOLATE CHIPS

1 CUP CHOPPED PECANS

Preheat oven to 350F (175C). Line a 15" x 10" jelly-roll pan with foil. In a medium bowl, beat together butter or margarine, brown sugar, egg yolk and vanilla until light and fluffy. Add flour and beat until blended. Spread mixture evenly into prepared pan. Bake 15 minutes, or until golden brown. Sprinkle chocolate chips over surface. Bake 2 to 3 minutes, or until chocolate melts. Remove from oven and let cool 1 minute. With a knife, spread melted chocolate evenly over top. Sprinkle with pecans. Cut in 54 squares and serve while warm.

Midnight Munchies

*A scrumptious combination of coconut, chocolate and
nuts in a layered cookie make a sensational midnight snack!*

1 (14-OZ.) CAN SWEETENED CONDENSED
   MILK
2 OUNCES UNSWEETENED CHOCOLATE
1-1/2 CUPS CHOPPED WALNUTS OR
   PECANS
1 CUP BUTTER OR MARGARINE, SOFTENED
1-1/4 CUPS PACKED DARK BROWN SUGAR
1/2 TABLESPOON VANILLA EXTRACT
1 TEASPOON ALMOND EXTRACT
2 CUPS ALL-PURPOSE FLOUR
1/2 TEASPOON BAKING SODA
2-1/2 CUPS ROLLED OATS

Preheat oven to 350F (175C). Grease a 13" x 9" baking pan. In a small saucepan over very low heat, melt condensed milk and chocolate, stirring constantly until smooth. Remove from heat, stir in nuts and set aside. In a medium bowl, beat together butter or margarine, brown sugar, vanilla and almond extract until light and fluffy. Add flour and baking soda, blending thoroughly. Stir in oats, mixing well. Press half of oat mixture evenly into bottom of prepared pan. Spread chocolate and nut mixture evenly on top. Press remaining oat mixture evenly on top. Bake 25 to 30 minutes, or until golden brown. Set on a wire rack and cool in pan. Cut in 54 bars.

Apricot Chocolate Chip Wonder Bars

*Apricot jam spread over rich chocolate chip batter and completed with crunchy
brown sugar crumb topping, then baked to perfection…these bars are pure heaven!*

3/4 CUP BUTTER OR MARGARINE,
    SOFTENED
3/4 CUP PACKED DARK BROWN SUGAR
2 TEASPOONS VANILLA EXTRACT
1-1/2 CUPS ALL-PURPOSE FLOUR
1 CUP SEMISWEET CHOCOLATE CHIPS
3/4 CUP CHOPPED WALNUTS (OPTIONAL)
1 CUP APRICOT JAM

❖

BROWN SUGAR CRUMB TOPPING
1 CUP ALL-PURPOSE FLOUR
1/2 CUP PACKED DARK BROWN SUGAR
1/3 CUP BUTTER OR MARGARINE,
    SOFTENED
1/2 CUP ROLLED OATS

Preheat oven to 350F (190C). Grease a 13" x 9" baking pan. In a large bowl, cream together butter or margarine and brown sugar until light and fluffy. Add vanilla and mix well. Stir in flour, blending thoroughly. Fold in chocolate chips and nuts, if desired. Press dough evenly into prepared pan. Spread apricot jam evenly over dough and set aside. Prepare Brown Sugar Crumb Topping. Sprinkle topping evenly over apricot jam. Bake 20 to 25 minutes, or until golden brown. Set on a wire rack and cool in pan. Cut in 32 bars.

Brown Sugar Crumb Topping

In a small bowl, combine flour and brown sugar, stirring until blended. Using a fork or pastry blender, cut in butter or margarine until size of peas. Stir in oats, blending thoroughly.

Variation #1: Add 1/2 teaspoon almond extract with vanilla. Omit chocolate chips and walnuts. Substitute 1 cup raspberry jam for apricot jam.

Variation #2: Decrease flour to 1-1/4 cups and sift into brown sugar mixture with 3 heaping tablespoons of cocoa powder. Decrease chocolate chips to 1/2 cup and add to dough with 1/2 cup white chocolate chips. Omit jam and crumb topping. Sprinkle cooled bars with powdered sugar.

Tangy Lemon Treats

Grandmother's favorite lemon bars!

2-1/2 CUPS ALL-PURPOSE FLOUR

1/2 CUP POWDERED SUGAR

1 CUP BUTTER OR MARGARINE, SOFTENED

4 EGGS

2 CUPS GRANULATED SUGAR

1/3 CUP LEMON JUICE

1/2 TEASPOON BAKING POWDER

POWDERED SUGAR

Preheat oven to 350F (175C). Lightly grease a 13" x 9" baking pan. In a large bowl, sift together 2 cups flour and powdered sugar. Cut in butter or margarine until mixture is the size of peas. Press mixture evenly into bottom of prepared pan and bake 20 to 25 minutes. In a medium bowl, beat together eggs, granulated sugar and lemon juice. Sift in remaining flour and baking powder. Stir until well mixed. Pour mixture over baked crust and bake an additional 25 minutes. Remove from oven and dust with powdered sugar. Set on a wire rack and cool in pan. Cut in 48 bars.

Peanut Butter & Jelly Picnic Packers

Peanut butter and jelly sandwiches never tasted this good!

1/2 CUP PEANUT BUTTER

1/4 CUP BUTTER OR MARGARINE,
SOFTENED

1/2 CUP PACKED DARK BROWN SUGAR

1 CUP ALL-PURPOSE FLOUR

❖

COCONUT-JAM TOPPING

1 EGG

1/2 CUP PACKED DARK BROWN SUGAR

1/3 CUP APRICOT JAM

1 TEASPOON VANILLA EXTRACT

2 TABLESPOONS ALL-PURPOSE FLOUR

1 TEASPOON BAKING POWDER

3/4 CUP FLAKED COCONUT

1 CUP WHITE CHOCOLATE CHIPS

Preheat oven to 350F (175C). Grease a 13" x 9" baking pan. In a medium bowl, combine peanut butter, butter or margarine and brown sugar, mixing until blended. Stir in flour. Spread dough evenly into prepared pan. Bake 10 minutes. While crust is baking, prepare Coconut-Jam Topping. Spread topping on baked crust. Return to oven; bake 25 minutes, or until golden brown. Set on a wire rack and cool in pan. Cut in 32 bars.

Coconut-Jam Topping

In a medium bowl, beat egg, brown sugar, jam and vanilla until blended. Mix in flour and baking powder. Stir in coconut and white chocolate chips.

Chocolate Mint Julep Bars

Mint chocolate chips and bourbon whiskey give these bars their unique, refreshing flavor.

1/2 CUP BUTTER OR MARGARINE

1-1/2 CUPS PACKED DARK BROWN SUGAR

2 TEASPOONS VANILLA EXTRACT

1/4 CUP BOURBON WHISKEY

1 EGG

1-1/4 CUPS ALL-PURPOSE FLOUR

1/2 TEASPOON BAKING SODA

1 (12-OZ.) BAG MINT CHOCOLATE CHIPS

2 TABLESPOONS POWDERED SUGAR

1 TABLESPOON UNSWEETENED COCOA
   POWDER

Preheat oven to 350F (175C). Grease a 9-inch-square baking pan. In a medium saucepan over low heat, melt butter or margarine. Remove from heat and allow to cool slightly. Place brown sugar in a medium bowl, stir in melted butter or margarine then vanilla. Whisk together bourbon and egg, and stir into sugar mixture blending until smooth. Stir in flour and baking soda, mixing well. Fold in mint chocolate chips. Spread into prepared pan. Bake 25 to 30 minutes or until a wooden pick inserted in center comes out barely moist with crumbs. Place pan on a wire rack and allow to cool. Combine powdered sugar and cocoa and dust bars lightly. Cut in 30 squares.

Chapter Five

---❖---

Holidays &
Special
Occasions

---❖---

Irresistible delicacies–that's what you'll find in this chapter of special brownie, blondie and bar cookie recipes—crafted to commemorate the religious, patriotic or sentimental days of the year. These unique recipes are sure to tempt and please guests year round!

Pumpkin Pie Bars

You've waited long enough with baited taste buds for November's pumpkin pie. Now relief is only a bar-cookie-bite away! Pumpkin, spices, pecans, butterscotch chips and caramel frosting highlight these year-round winners.

1 EGG

1/2 CUP BUTTER OR MARGARINE, MELTED

3 TABLESPOONS MILK

1 CUP PACKED DARK BROWN SUGAR

1/4 CUP HONEY

1 CUP PUMPKIN PIE FILLING

2 CUPS ALL-PURPOSE FLOUR

1/2 TEASPOON BAKING SODA

1 TEASPOON GROUND CINNAMON

1/2 TEASPOON GROUND GINGER

1/4 TEASPOON GROUND ALLSPICE

1/4 TEASPOON GROUND CLOVES

3/4 CUP CHOPPED PECANS

3/4 CUP BUTTERSCOTCH CHIPS

❖

CARAMEL FROSTING

1/2 CUP BUTTER OR MARGARINE

1 CUP PACKED DARK BROWN SUGAR

1/4 CUP MILK

2 CUPS POWDERED SUGAR

Preheat oven to 350F (175C). Grease a 13" x 9" baking pan. In a large bowl, cream egg, melted butter or margarine, milk, brown sugar, honey and pumpkin pie filling until light and fluffy. Set aside. In a medium bowl, stir together flour, baking soda, cinnamon, ginger, allspice and cloves. Gently fold dry ingredients into pumpkin mixture, stirring until blended. Fold in chopped pecans and butterscotch chips. Pour into prepared pan. Bake 25 to 30 minutes, or until a wooden pick inserted in center comes out barely moist with crumbs. Set on a wire rack and cool in pan. Prepare Caramel Frosting. Spread frosting over cooled bars. Allow to set, at least one hour before cutting. Cut in 32 bars.

Caramel Frosting

In a medium saucepan over low heat, melt butter or margarine. Stir in brown sugar. Heat to boiling, stirring constantly. Boil and stir 2 minutes. Stir in milk. Heat to boiling again, stirring constantly. Remove from heat and cool to lukewarm. Gradually blend in powdered sugar. Place pan of frosting in bowl of cold water. Beat until smooth and of spreading consistency. If frosting becomes too stiff, add additional milk, 1 teaspoon at a time.

Pumpkin Spice Bars

These pielike bar cookies are sure to be a welcome addition to the Thanksgiving table of treats.

1 CUP ALL-PURPOSE FLOUR

1 TEASPOON PUMPKIN PIE SPICE

1 TEASPOON GROUND NUTMEG

1/2 TEASPOON BAKING SODA

1 CUP CANNED PUMPKIN

1 EGG

1/2 CUP BUTTER OR MARGARINE,
    SOFTENED

1-1/2 CUPS PACKED DARK BROWN SUGAR

1 TABLESPOON VANILLA EXTRACT

❖

STREUSEL TOPPING

3/4 CUP ALL-PURPOSE FLOUR

1/2 CUP BUTTER OR MARGARINE, MELTED

2/3 CUP PACKED BROWN SUGAR

1/2 CUP PECANS, CHOPPED

1 TEASPOON GROUND CINNAMON

1/2 TEASPOON PUMPKIN PIE SPICE

❖

ICING

1/2 CUP POWDERED SUGAR

2-1/2 TEASPOONS MILK

Preheat oven to 375F (190C). Grease 10" x 7" or a 9-inch-square baking pan. In a small bowl, combine flour, pumpkin pie spice, nutmeg and baking soda. Set aside. In a large bowl, beat together pumpkin and egg until light and fluffy. Stir in butter or margarine, brown sugar and vanilla. Gradually add flour mixture and mix thoroughly. Spread batter into prepared pan and set aside. Prepare Streusel Topping. Pour over batter. With a spatula, spread streusel mixture to cover completely. Bake 25 to 30 minutes, or until golden brown. Set on a wire rack and cool in pan completely before cutting in squares. Prepare Icing. Drizzle over cooled bars.

Streusel Topping
In a small bowl, combine all ingredients.

Icing
Mix together powdered sugar and milk until smooth. If icing is too thick, gradually add more milk, one teaspoon at a time, until icing is of desired consistency.

Gingerbread Gems

Tangy lemon glaze finishes off these not-too-sweet, yet oh-so-delicious and nutritious gingerbread bars. They're the perfect holiday treat.

2 CUPS ALL-PURPOSE FLOUR

1/2 CUP ROLLED OATS

1/2 CUP PACKED DARK BROWN SUGAR

1 TEASPOON BAKING SODA

1 TEASPOON GROUND CINNAMON

1 TEASPOON GROUND GINGER

1/2 TEASPOON GROUND ALLSPICE

1/2 CUP GOLDEN RAISINS

1 CUP DARK MOLASSES

1/2 CUP BOILING WATER

1/4 CUP WHIPPING CREAM

1 EGG

❖

LEMON GLAZE

1-1/2 CUPS POWDERED SUGAR

2 TABLESPOONS WHIPPING CREAM

2 TABLESPOONS LEMON JUICE

Preheat oven to 350F (175C). Grease a 13" x 9" baking pan. In a large bowl, combine flour, oats, brown sugar, baking soda, cinnamon, ginger, allspice and raisins until blended. Add molasses, water, cream and egg and mix until thoroughly blended. Pour into prepared pan. Bake 25 to 30 minutes or until a wooden pick inserted in center comes out clean. Set on a wire rack and cool in pan. While still warm, cut in 42 bars. Prepare Lemon Glaze. Drizzle glaze over cut bars so glaze seeps into cracks. Cool completely before removing from pan.

Lemon Glaze
In a small bowl, mix all ingredients until blended.

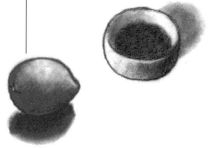

Boston Cream Pie Brownies

"Luscious" best describes these cream-filled, chocolate-topped brownies. They're simply sinful in the tradition of Boston Cream Pie!

4 OUNCES UNSWEETENED CHOCOLATE

1/2 CUP SEMISWEET CHOCOLATE CHIPS

1 CUP BUTTER OR MARGARINE

1-3/4 CUPS ALL-PURPOSE FLOUR

3/4 CUP UNSWEETENED COCOA POWDER

1 TEASPOON BAKING POWDER

1 CUP PACKED DARK BROWN SUGAR

1 CUP GRANULATED SUGAR

1/2 CUP VEGETABLE OIL

2 EGGS

2/3 CUP COLD WATER

2 TABLESPOONS VANILLA EXTRACT

1 CUP CHOPPED NUTS (OPTIONAL)

❖

CREAM FILLING

2 TABLESPOONS ALL-PURPOSE FLOUR

1/3 CUP GRANULATED SUGAR

1 EGG

3/4 CUP SCALDED MILK

1 TEASPOON VANILLA EXTRACT

1/2 CUP WHIPPING CREAM, WHIPPED

❖

THIN CHOCOLATE COATING

2 TABLESPOONS BUTTER OR MARGARINE

2 OUNCES UNSWEETENED CHOCOLATE

1 CUP POWDERED SUGAR, SIFTED

2 TABLESPOONS BOILING WATER

Preheat oven to 350F (175C). Grease and flour two 9-inch-round baking pans. In a small saucepan over low heat, melt unsweetened chocolate, semisweet chocolate chips and butter or margarine, stirring until smooth. Remove from heat and let cool to lukewarm. Sift flour, cocoa and baking powder into a small bowl. Set aside. In a large bowl, combine sugars. Stir in cooled chocolate mixture, blending well. Whisk together oil, eggs, water and vanilla, then add to chocolate mixture. Stir in flour mixture, blending well. Fold in nuts, if desired. Spread batter into prepared pans. Bake 20 to 25 minutes, or until a wooden pick inserted in center comes out barely moist. Cool 5 minutes in pans. Carefully remove brownie layers from pans and set on wire racks to cool. Prepare Cream Filling. Makes 16 servings.

Cream Filling

In the top of a double boiler, combine flour and sugar. Stir in egg, then scalded milk. Blend thoroughly. Cook 5 minutes over boiling water, stirring constantly. Cook 5 minutes longer, stirring occasionally. Filling should be thick. Remove from heat and refrigerate until cold, at least 30 minutes. Filling will thicken as it cools. When cool, add vanilla, then whip and fold in cream. Spread between cooled brownie layers. Prepare Thin Chocolate Coating. Drizzle over filled brownie layers. Refrigerate until ready to serve.

Thin Chocolate Coating

In a small saucepan over low heat, melt butter or margarine and chocolate, stirring until smooth. Remove from heat and add powdered sugar, stirring until well blended. Return to heat and add boiling water, stirring until smooth. If necessary, add more water to achieve spreading consistency.

Crème de la Crème Brownies

Velvety smooth, these deep, dark brownies get their rich flavor from loads of chocolate, chocolate-flavored liqueur, French vanilla cream pudding in the batter and chocolate frosting on top!

PUDDING

1/3 CUP GRANULATED SUGAR

2 TABLESPOONS CORNSTARCH

2 CUPS MILK

2 EGG YOLKS, BEATEN

2 TABLESPOONS BUTTER OR MARGARINE,
  SOFTENED

2 TEASPOONS VANILLA EXTRACT

❖

BROWNIE

5 OUNCES UNSWEETENED CHOCOLATE

1 CUP BUTTER OR MARGARINE, SOFTENED

1-3/4 CUPS PACKED DARK BROWN SUGAR

4 EGGS

3 TABLESPOONS WHIPPING CREAM

1 TABLESPOON VANILLA EXTRACT

1/2 CUP CRÈME DE CACAO LIQUEUR

1-1/4 CUPS ALL-PURPOSE FLOUR

❖

CHOCOLATE ICING

2 TABLESPOONS BUTTER OR MARGARINE

2 OUNCES UNSWEETENED CHOCOLATE

1 TEASPOON VANILLA EXTRACT

1 CUP SIFTED POWDERED SUGAR

2 TABLESPOONS CRÈME DE CACAO
  LIQUEUR

HOT WATER, AS NECESSARY

Pudding

Mix sugar and cornstarch in a large saucepan. Gradually stir in milk. Cook over medium heat, stirring constantly, until mixture thickens and boils, about 5 minutes. Boil 1 minute, stirring constantly. In a separate bowl, stir half of pudding mixture into beaten egg yolks; then stir back into pudding mixture in saucepan. Bring to a boil and stir 1 minute; remove from heat. Stir in butter or margarine and vanilla, mixing well. Set aside to cool and prepare Brownie.

Brownie

Preheat oven to 350F (175C). Grease 13" x 9" baking pan. In a small saucepan over low heat, melt chocolate. Set aside to cool. In a large bowl, cream butter or margarine and brown sugar until light and fluffy. Using a wire whisk, beat in eggs, one at a time. Blend in chocolate, then whipping cream, vanilla and crème de cacao, mixing thoroughly. Stir in flour, mixing well. Spread batter into prepared pan. Spread pudding evenly over top, and then swirl into batter with a knife. Bake 25 to 30 minutes, or until a wooden pick inserted in center comes out barely moist and pudding is slightly firm. Set on a wire rack and cool in pan. Prepare Chocolate Icing. Drizzle icing over brownies. Let stand until icing sets, at least 2 hours. Cut in 32 squares. Store in refrigerator.

Chocolate Icing

In a small saucepan over low heat, melt butter or margarine and chocolate, stirring until smooth. Remove from heat and add vanilla, then sifted powdered sugar, stirring until blended. Return to heat and add crème de cacao, stirring until smooth and silky. If necessary, add hot water, a teaspoon at a time, to achieve spreading consistency.

Chocolate-Raspberry Hot Fudge Browndaes

Here's the ultimate chocolate lover's dessert–chocolate chip brownies topped with the ice cream of your choice and finished off with creamy hot fudge, whipped cream and other garnishes of your choice!

BROWNIE

10 TABLESPOONS BUTTER OR MARGARINE

1 CUP PACKED DARK BROWN SUGAR

1 EGG

3 TABLESPOONS DARK CORN SYRUP

1 TABLESPOON VANILLA EXTRACT

1/2 TEASPOON ALMOND EXTRACT

3/4 CUP ALL-PURPOSE FLOUR

1/2 CUP UNSWEETENED COCOA POWDER

1/2 TEASPOON BAKING POWDER

1 CUP SEMISWEET CHOCOLATE CHIPS

2 PINTS ICE CREAM

❖

HOT FUDGE SAUCE

1-1/2 CUPS WHIPPING CREAM

1-1/2 CUPS SUGAR

3 OUNCES UNSWEETENED CHOCOLATE

4 TABLESPOONS BUTTER OR MARGARINE,
    CUT INTO PIECES

1/2 TABLESPOON VANILLA EXTRACT

1/2 TABLESPOON RASPBERRY-FLAVORED
    LIQUEUR

❖

GARNISHES (OPTIONAL)

WHIPPED CREAM

SHAVED SEMISWEET CHOCOLATE

FRESH RASPBERRIES

Brownie

Preheat oven to 350F (175C). Grease a 9-inch-round springform pan. In a large bowl, cream together butter or margarine and brown sugar. Whisk together egg, corn syrup, vanilla and almond extracts and add to sugar mixture, blending thoroughly. Sift flour, cocoa and baking powder into a small bowl, then gradually add to creamed mixture, stirring well. Fold in chocolate chips. Spread batter into prepared pan. Bake 30 to 35 minutes, or until a wooden pick inserted in center comes out barely moist. Set on a wire rack and cool in pan. Do not remove outer edge of pan. When brownie is cool, spread ice cream evenly over brownie. Cover with foil or plastic wrap and freeze. Thirty minutes before serving, remove the pan from the freezer and let sit at room temperature to soften slightly. Prepare Hot Fudge Sauce. Wrap a hot towel around the springform pan to loosen edges. Remove sides. Cut the pie in 8 wedges, and generously pour hot fudge over each serving. Garnish with whipped cream, fresh raspberries and shaved chocolate, if desired.

Hot Fudge Sauce

In a heavy saucepan, combine whipping cream, sugar and chocolate. Cook over medium heat, stirring constantly, until sugar dissolves and chocolate melts. Stir in butter or margarine, and reduce heat to low. Continue cooking, stirring occasionally, until the sauce is thick, 5 to 7 minutes. Stir in vanilla and raspberry liqueur. Remove from heat.

Spicy Mincemeat Bars

The perfect holiday treat, these fruit-filled bars get better with
age (only a day or so) just like traditional Christmas puddings and fruitcakes.

2 CUPS ALL-PURPOSE FLOUR
1/2 TEASPOON BAKING POWDER
1/2 TEASPOON BAKING SODA
1/2 TEASPOON GROUND CINNAMON
1/2 CUP BUTTER OR MARGARINE,
    SOFTENED
1/2 CUP PACKED DARK BROWN SUGAR
1/3 CUP DARK MOLASSES
1 EGG
2 TABLESPOONS APRICOT-FLAVORED
    BRANDY
1 CUP PREPARED MINCEMEAT
1/2 CUP GOLDEN RAISINS
3/4 CUP CHOPPED WALNUTS OR PECANS

❖

CARAMEL FROSTING
1/2 CUP BUTTER OR MARGARINE
1 CUP PACKED DARK BROWN SUGAR
2 TABLESPOONS MILK
2 TABLESPOONS APRICOT-FLAVORED
    BRANDY
2 CUPS POWDERED SUGAR

Preheat oven to 350F (175C). Grease a 13" x 9" pan. Sift flour, baking powder, baking soda and cinnamon in a small bowl, set aside. In a large bowl, cream butter or margarine, sugar, molasses and egg until light and fluffy. Blend in brandy and mincemeat, mixing well. Gradually add flour mixture, mixing until thoroughly blended. Fold in raisins and nuts. Spread batter evenly into prepared pan. Bake 25 to 30 minutes, or until a wooden pick inserted in center comes out barely moist. Set on a wire rack and cool in pan. Prepare Caramel Frosting. Frost bars and set aside until firm. Cut in 35 bars.

Caramel Frosting

In a medium saucepan over low heat, melt butter or margarine. Stir in brown sugar. Heat to boiling, stirring constantly. Boil and stir 2 minutes; stir in milk and brandy. Heat to boiling and boil 1 minute, remove from heat and cool to lukewarm. Gradually stir in powdered sugar. Place saucepan in a bowl of cold water; beat until smooth and of spreading consistency. If frosting becomes too thick, stir in more milk, a teaspoon at a time, until desired consistency is achieved.

Mint Waferettes

A delicious blondie bottom topped with a mint wafer and chocolate-flavored liqueur topping is guaranteed to please. These delectable minty treats are just as perfect on a party platter as in a brown bag lunch.

1-1/4 CUPS BUTTER OR MARGARINE,
    SOFTENED
1 CUP PACKED DARK BROWN SUGAR
1/2 CUP GRANULATED SUGAR
2 EGGS
2 TABLESPOONS VANILLA EXTRACT
2-1/2 CUPS ALL-PURPOSE FLOUR
1 TEASPOON BAKING SODA
6 OUNCES (36) MINT WAFERS
2/3 CUP CHOCOLATE-FLAVORED LIQUEUR
1-1/2 CUPS SEMISWEET CHOCOLATE CHIPS

Preheat oven to 350F (175C). Grease a 13" x 9" baking pan. In a large bowl, cream 1 cup butter or margarine and the sugars until light and fluffy. Add eggs and 1 tablespoon vanilla, blending well. Add flour and baking soda, stirring thoroughly. Spread batter into prepared pan. Bake 20 minutes, or until golden brown. Remove from oven and top immediately with mint wafers. Return to oven 2 to 5 minutes, or until wafers are softened. Remove from oven and gently spread wafers with a knife. In a medium saucepan over low heat combine liqueur, chocolate chips, remaining butter or margarine and vanilla. Melt, stirring until thoroughly blended. Spread evenly over mint wafers. Return to oven and bake 8 more minutes. Set on a wire rack and cool in pan. Cut in 40 bars.

Lemon-Coconut Dessert Bars

*Tangy and sweet lemon-coconut flavor makes these fresh-tasting
bars the perfect, sophisticated ending to an afternoon tea or shower.*

COOKIE CRUST

1-1/2 CUPS ALL-PURPOSE FLOUR

1/2 CUP PACKED DARK BROWN SUGAR

1/2 CUP BUTTER OR MARGARINE,
    SOFTENED

❖

LEMON-COCONUT FILLING

1 EGG

1 TEASPOON VANILLA EXTRACT

3 TABLESPOONS LEMON JUICE

1 TEASPOON GRATED LEMON PEEL

1 CUP PACKED DARK BROWN SUGAR

1-1/2 CUPS FLAKED COCONUT

3 TABLESPOONS ALL-PURPOSE FLOUR

❖

LEMON GLAZE

1 CUP SIFTED POWDERED SUGAR

1 TABLESPOON BUTTER OR MARGARINE,
    MELTED

JUICE OF 1 MEDIUM LEMON

Cookie Crust

Preheat oven to 275F (135C). Grease a 13" x 9" baking pan. In a medium bowl, combine flour, brown sugar and butter or margarine, blending thoroughly. Pat evenly into prepared pan. Bake 10 minutes. Remove from oven; set aside. Increase oven temperature to 350F (175C). Prepare Lemon-Coconut Filling. Spread on top of baked crust. Return to oven and bake 20 minutes. Place on wire rack and cool in pan. Prepare Lemon Glaze. While still warm, cut cookies in 24 bars. Drizzle glaze over top. Complete cooling. Store in refrigerator.

Lemon-Coconut Filling

In a medium bowl, combine all ingredients; blend well.

Lemon Glaze

In a small bowl, combine all ingredients, blending until all powdered sugar lumps disappear and mixture resembles thick cream.

Eggnog Brownies

Ring in the holidays with these brandy-flavored eggnog brownies.

2 OUNCES UNSWEETENED CHOCOLATE

1/4 CUP SEMISWEET CHOCOLATE CHIPS

2/3 CUP BUTTER OR MARGARINE

1-1/4 CUPS ALL-PURPOSE FLOUR

1/4 CUP UNSWEETENED COCOA POWDER

1/4 TEASPOON BAKING POWDER

1 CUP PACKED DARK BROWN SUGAR

1 EGG

1/3 CUP HEAVY CREAM

2 TEASPOONS VANILLA EXTRACT

1 TABLESPOON BRANDY (OR BRANDY
   EXTRACT)

NUTMEG

❖

CREAMY GLAZE

1/4 CUP BUTTER OR MARGARINE

1-1/2 CUPS SIFTED POWDERED SUGAR

1 TEASPOON VANILLA EXTRACT

1 TEASPOON BRANDY EXTRACT

2 TO 3 TABLESPOONS WHIPPING CREAM

Preheat oven to 350F (175C). Grease a 9-inch-square baking pan. In a small saucepan over low heat, melt unsweetened chocolate, semisweet chocolate chips and butter or margarine, stirring until smooth. Remove from heat and let cool to lukewarm. In a small bowl, sift flour, cocoa and baking powder. Set aside. In a large bowl, combine brown sugar and cooled chocolate mixture, blending well. Whisk egg, heavy cream, vanilla and brandy extract together and add to chocolate mixture, beating thoroughly. Stir in flour mixture, beating 50 strokes by hand. Spread into prepared pan. Bake 18 to 22 minutes, or until a wooden pick inserted in center comes out barely moist. Set on a wire rack and cool in pan. Prepare Creamy Glaze; drizzle evenly over warm brownies. Sprinkle lightly with nutmeg. Cut in 25 squares.

Creamy Glaze

In a small saucepan, melt butter or margarine until golden brown. Add powdered sugar, vanilla and brandy extracts, combining thoroughly. Stir in heavy cream, 1 tablespoon at a time, until glaze is of desired spreading consistency.

Pineapple-Apricot Dessert Bars

*A tropical treat, these easy bars feature yellow cake mix, pineapple, chocolate chips
and apricot-brandy cream pudding…what a combination!*

1 (18.25-OZ.) BOX YELLOW CAKE MIX

1 (8-OZ.) CAN PINEAPPLE CHUNKS IN JUICE
  (UNDRAINED)

1/3 CUP SEMISWEET CHOCOLATE CHIPS

3/4 CUP BUTTER OR MARGARINE, MELTED

❖

APRICOT-BRANDY CREAM PUDDING

1 CUP SUGAR

2 TABLESPOONS CORNSTARCH

2 CUPS MILK

2 EGG YOLKS, SLIGHTLY BEATEN

2 TABLESPOONS APRICOT BRANDY

1 TEASPOON VANILLA EXTRACT

1 TABLESPOON BUTTER OR MARGARINE

Preheat oven to 350F (175C). Grease a 13" x 9" baking pan.
Prepare Apricot-Brandy Cream Pudding first; set aside. Dump dry
cake mix in prepared pan, spread evenly. Top with pineapple
chunks and chocolate chips, distributing evenly. Spoon on
pudding, covering entire mixture. Pour melted butter over top.
Bake 45 to 50 minutes, or until a wooden pick inserted in center
comes out barely moist with crumbs and pudding has set. Set on a
wire rack and cool in pan. Cut in 30 bars. Keep refrigerated.

Apricot-Brandy Cream Pudding

In a medium saucepan, combine sugar and cornstarch. Stir in milk.
Stir constantly over low heat until thickened and bubbly, about 5
minutes. Cook and stir 2 minutes more. Remove from heat. Stir a
small amount of hot mixture into beaten egg yolks. Add egg yolk
mixture to remaining mixture in saucepan. Cook and stir 2 minutes
more. Remove from heat. Stir in brandy, vanilla and butter or
margarine.

Mexican Chocolate Brownie Pie

This chocolate-cinnamon flavor combination is a guaranteed winner.

3 OUNCES CREAM CHEESE, SOFTENED

1/2 CUP BUTTER OR MARGARINE,
 SOFTENED

2 TEASPOONS VANILLA EXTRACT

1 TEASPOON GROUND CINNAMON

1/4 CUP GRANULATED SUGAR

1/4 CUP UNSWEETENED COCOA POWDER

1-1/2 CUPS ALL-PURPOSE FLOUR

❖

FILLING

2 OUNCES UNSWEETENED CHOCOLATE

1/4 CUP BUTTER OR MARGARINE

1 CUP FIRMLY PACKED DARK BROWN
 SUGAR

1/4 CUP LIGHT CORN SYRUP

2 TEASPOONS VANILLA EXTRACT

2 EGGS

1/4 CUP WHIPPING CREAM

❖

GARNISHES (OPTIONAL)

ICE CREAM

WHIPPED CREAM

CHOCOLATE SAUCE

Preheat oven to 350F (175C). In a medium bowl, beat cream cheese, butter or margarine and vanilla until smooth. Add cinnamon, sugar, cocoa and flour, beating until dough begins to cling together in a ball. Roll pastry in a circle 3 inches larger than a 9-inch pie plate. Push pastry down into pan and flute edges. Set aside. Prepare Filling. Pour filling into prepared crust, and bake 50 minutes or until filling is puffy and barely dry. Filling will sink as it cools. Cool at least 4 hours before serving. Serve with ice cream, whipped cream or chocolate sauce, if desired. Store in refrigerator. Cut in 8 wedges.

Filling

In a medium saucepan over low heat, melt chocolate and butter or margarine, stirring constantly. Remove from heat. Stir in brown sugar, corn syrup and vanilla. Add eggs and whipping cream; beat well.

Pecan Pie Bars

Traditional pecan pie made into delicious and easy-to-make bar cookies.

2 CUPS ALL-PURPOSE FLOUR

1/2 CUP POWDERED SUGAR

1 CUP BUTTER OR MARGARINE, SOFTENED

3 EGGS

1 CUP DARK CORN SYRUP

1 CUP GRANULATED SUGAR

2 TABLESPOONS BUTTER OR MARGARINE,
   SOFTENED

1 TEASPOON VANILLA EXTRACT

1-1/2 CUPS CHOPPED PECANS

Preheat oven to 350F (175C). Lightly grease a 13" x 9" baking pan. Sift flour and powdered sugar into a large bowl. Cut in butter or margarine until mixture is the size of peas. Press mixture evenly in bottom of prepared pan. In a small bowl, lightly beat eggs. In a large bowl, combine corn syrup, sugar, butter or margarine and vanilla. Stir until blended. Add beaten eggs, vanilla and pecans and pour over crust. Bake 50 to 55 minutes, or until knife inserted halfway between center and edge comes out clean. Set on a wire rack and cool in pan. Cut in 32 bars.

S' Mores

*A twist on a chocolatey-marshmallow campfire favorite—this bar cookie
version is equally at home in a lunch box or as an around-the-campfire treat.*

1/2 CUP BUTTER OR MARGARINE

2 CUPS GRAHAM CRACKER CRUMBS

1-1/2 CUPS SEMISWEET CHOCOLATE CHIPS

1 (14-OZ.) CAN SWEETENED CONDENSED
   MILK

2 CUPS MINIATURE MARSHMALLOWS

Preheat oven to 350F (175C). Melt butter or margarine in the bottom of a 9-inch-square baking pan. Using the back of a spoon, carefully press graham cracker crumbs into butter or margarine, forming a crust. Sprinkle chocolate chips evenly over top. Drizzle condensed milk over chocolate chips. Bake 30 minutes. Remove from oven and sprinkle marshmallows evenly over top. Broil in oven 3 minutes, or until marshmallows are barely browned. Set on a wire rack and cool in pan. Cut in 16 to 25 bars.

Romance Tea Bars

This bar cookie is as pretty as it is delectable!

1 CUP BUTTER OR MARGARINE, SOFTENED

2 CUPS PLUS 2 TABLESPOONS ALL-
   PURPOSE FLOUR

1/4 CUP GRANULATED SUGAR

2 EGGS

1-1/2 CUPS PACKED DARK BROWN SUGAR

3/4 TEASPOON BAKING POWDER

1 TEASPOON VANILLA EXTRACT

1/2 CUP SHREDDED COCONUT

1 CUP COARSELY CHOPPED WALNUTS

POWDERED SUGAR

Preheat oven to 350F (175C). In a large bowl, cream butter or margarine until soft. Blend in 2 cups flour and granulated sugar. Spread mixture evenly into ungreased 15" x 10" jelly-roll pan. Bake 10 minutes. While cookie layer is baking, in a medium bowl, beat eggs until light and fluffy. Stir in brown sugar, remaining flour, baking powder and vanilla. Beat until thick and smooth. Fold in coconut and walnuts. Spread evenly over baked crust. Bake 20 minutes, or until golden brown and firm. Do not overcook. Set on a wire rack and cool in pan. Dust with powdered sugar. Cut in 32 bars.

Brownie Sundae Loaf

A hot fudge sundae rolled into a brownie loaf makes
this a unique dessert that will be enjoyed over and over again.

3 OUNCES UNSWEETENED CHOCOLATE

3/4 CUP BUTTER OR MARGARINE

1-1/2 CUPS SUGAR

1 CUP BUTTERMILK BISCUIT MIX

3/4 CUP CHOPPED WALNUTS OR PECANS

1-1/2 TEASPOONS VANILLA EXTRACT

3 EGGS

1 QUART VANILLA, CHOCOLATE OR
   COFFEE ICE CREAM, SLIGHTLY
   SOFTENED

POWDERED SUGAR

❖

GARNISHES

HOT FUDGE SAUCE

WHIPPED CREAM

Preheat oven to 350F (175C). Line a 15" x 10" jelly-roll pan with foil. Grease foil. In a small saucepan over low heat, melt chocolate and butter or margarine. Set aside. In a large bowl, mix sugar, biscuit mix, nuts, vanilla, eggs and melted chocolate mixture together. Stir vigorously 30 strokes. Spread evenly into prepared pan. Bake 25 minutes. Set on a wire rack and cool in pan. Invert brownie on cookie sheet and remove foil. Cut brownie crosswise into 3 equal parts. Place one part of brownie on serving platter and spread with half of ice cream. Top with another brownie part, remaining ice cream and third brownie part. Sprinkle with powdered sugar. Wrap in aluminum foil and freeze until firm, at least 8 hours. Remove from freezer 10 minutes before serving. Cut into slices. Serve with hot fudge sauce and whipped cream. Makes 8 to 10 servings.

Fudge Brownies with White Chocolate Sauce

*Interesting and absolutely delectable, apricot-flavored white
chocolate sauce tops fudge brownie squares…this is a true dessert delight!*

4 OUNCES UNSWEETENED CHOCOLATE
3/4 CUP BUTTER OR MARGARINE
3 EGGS
1/4 CUP BUTTERMILK
2 TEASPOONS VANILLA EXTRACT
1-1/2 CUPS SUGAR
1 CUP ALL-PURPOSE FLOUR
1/4 TEASPOON BAKING SODA
1/2 CUP CHOPPED WALNUTS

❖

WHITE CHOCOLATE SAUCE
1/3 CUP BUTTER OR MARGARINE
1/2 CUP WATER
3 OUNCES WHITE CHOCOLATE
2 TABLESPOONS LIGHT CORN SYRUP
1/2 CUP APRICOT PRESERVES

Preheat oven to 350F (175C). Grease and flour a 13" x 9" baking pan. In a small saucepan over low heat, melt chocolate and butter or margarine. Set aside. In a large bowl, beat eggs 1 minute. Blend in buttermilk and beat 1 minute more. Add melted chocolate mixture, beating well. Add vanilla, then sugar, blending thoroughly. Stir together flour and baking soda and add to chocolate mixture. Fold in walnuts. Spread into prepared pan. Bake 25 to 30 minutes, or until a wooden pick comes out barely moist with crumbs. Set on a wire rack and cool in pan. Prepare White Chocolate Sauce. Cut in 24 squares. Top with warm sauce.

White Chocolate Sauce

In a medium saucepan, melt butter or margarine in water. Bring to a boil, stirring constantly. Reduce heat to low, add white chocolate, stirring until smooth. Add corn syrup and preserves. Bring to a boil and cook gently about 5 minutes, stirring frequently. Serve warm. Store sauce in refrigerator. May be reheated. Makes about 1 cup.

Holiday Fruit Bars

Four different dried fruits and delicate orange flavoring combine to make these favorite holiday treats.

1 CUP BUTTER OR MARGARINE, SOFTENED
1 CUP PACKED DARK BROWN SUGAR
1 TABLESPOON VANILLA EXTRACT
2 CUPS ALL-PURPOSE FLOUR
1/2 CUP FINELY CHOPPED DRIED
    APRICOTS
1/2 CUP FINELY CHOPPED DRIED FIGS OR
    PRUNES
1/2 CUP CHOPPED DATES
1 CUP RAISINS
1 CUP CHOPPED PECANS

❖

ORANGE GLAZE
1 TABLESPOON BUTTER OR MARGARINE,
    MELTED
1/2 CUP POWDERED SUGAR, SIFTED
1 TABLESPOON ORANGE-FLAVORED
    LIQUEUR
1 TEASPOON GRATED ORANGE PEEL
1 TEASPOON WATER

Preheat oven to 350F (175C). Grease a 13" x 9" baking pan. In a large bowl, combine butter or margarine, brown sugar and vanilla, beating until light and fluffy. Stir in flour, blending well. Fold in dried fruits and nuts, mixing thoroughly. Spread mixture into prepared pan. Bake 25 to 30 minutes, or until golden brown. Set on a wire rack and allow to cool in pan. Meanwhile, prepare Orange Glaze. Drizzle over warm cookies. Cut in 36 bars.

Orange Glaze

In a small bowl, combine melted butter or margarine, powdered sugar, liqueur, orange peel and water until smooth.

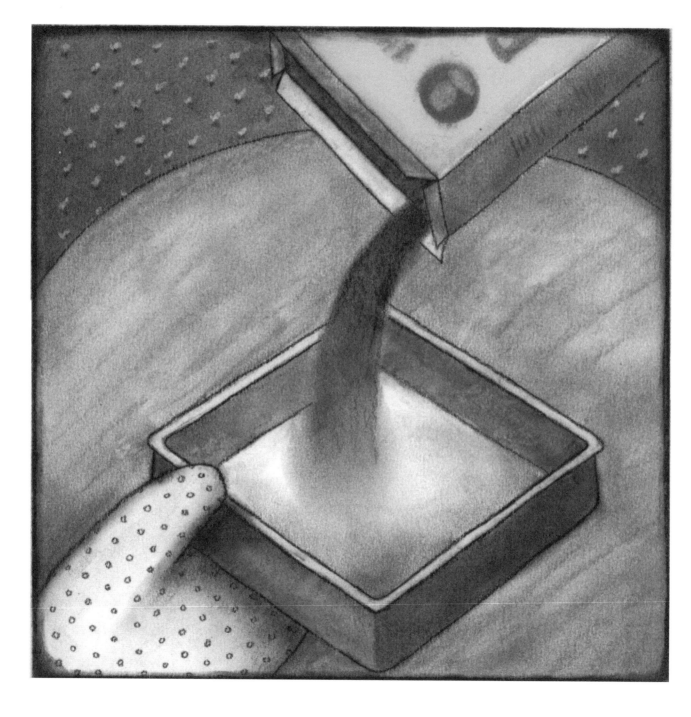

Chapter Six

❖

Quick
&
Easy

❖

How often do you wish you had a batch of warm, freshly-baked cookies to serve drop-in guests or neighborhood kids? In this chapter, you'll find loads of recipes that can be prepared quickly and easily. Some recipes use packaged baking mixes that you can keep handy in the pantry, while others are made from scratch using time-saving methods. There are even recipes that don't have to be baked at all! Whatever the recipe one thing is sure—it's going to be a snap to bake and equally quick to disappear!

Applesauce Bars

Easy-to-make bar cookies that disappear in no time. Perfect for snack attacks and they're healthy, too!

1/3 CUP BUTTER OR MARGARINE

1 CUP PACKED DARK BROWN SUGAR

1/2 CUP APPLESAUCE

1 EGG

2 TEASPOONS VANILLA EXTRACT

1-1/4 CUPS ALL-PURPOSE FLOUR

1 TEASPOON BAKING POWDER

1/4 TEASPOON BAKING SODA

1 TEASPOON GROUND CINNAMON

1/4 TEASPOON GROUND ALLSPICE

3/4 CUP RAISINS

3/4 CUP CHOPPED WALNUTS (OPTIONAL)

❖

CARAMEL GLAZE

1/2 CUP BUTTER OR MARGARINE

1 CUP PACKED DARK BROWN SUGAR

1/4 CUP MILK

1 TEASPOON VANILLA EXTRACT

Preheat oven to 350F (175C). Grease a 13" x 9" baking pan. In a medium saucepan over low heat, melt butter or margarine. Remove from heat. Stir in brown sugar, applesauce, egg and vanilla, mixing well. Add flour, baking powder, baking soda, cinnamon and allspice, blending thoroughly. Stir in raisins and walnuts, if desired. Spread batter evenly into prepared pan. Bake 23 to 25 minutes, or until a wooden pick inserted in center comes out clean. Cool on a wire rack, then cut in 35 bars; leave in pan. Prepare Caramel Glaze. While warm, pour glaze over cut cookies, allowing glaze to seep into cracks and crevices. When glaze has set, bars are ready to serve. Makes 35 bars.

Caramel Glaze

In a medium saucepan over low heat, melt butter or margarine. Stir in brown sugar. Heat to boiling and boil 1 minute, stirring constantly. Boil and stir 2 minutes; stir in milk and vanilla. Heat to boiling, remove from heat and cool to lukewarm.

Dark Chocolate Cake Brownies

Whip these up in minutes–mix and bake in the same pan! The secret here
is cider vinegar–it makes these cakelike brownies lusciously dark and moist.

1-1/2 CUPS ALL-PURPOSE FLOUR

1 CUP SUGAR

3 HEAPING TABLESPOONS UNSWEETENED
    COCOA POWDER

1 TEASPOON BAKING SODA

1 TABLESPOON VANILLA EXTRACT

6 TABLESPOONS BUTTER OR MARGARINE,
    MELTED

1 TABLESPOON CIDER VINEGAR

1 CUP COLD WATER

1 CUP SEMISWEET CHOCOLATE CHIPS

POWDERED SUGAR

Preheat oven to 350F (175C). Sift flour, sugar, cocoa and baking soda into an ungreased 9-inch-square baking pan. Make three depressions in dry ingredients. Add vanilla in one depression, melted butter or margarine in another and vinegar in the third. Pour cold water over top. Stir until blended. Fold in chocolate chips. Bake 30 to 35 minutes, or until a wooden pick inserted in the center comes out clean. Set on a wire rack and cool in pan. Dust with powdered sugar or top with your favorite fudge frosting. Cut in 25 squares.

Chewy Butterscotch Blondies

As easy as 1,2,3 and so delicious, too. They're packed with oats and butterscotch chips!

1-1/4 CUPS PACKED DARK BROWN SUGAR

2/3 CUP BUTTER OR MARGARINE,
    SOFTENED

1-1/3 CUPS ROLLED OATS

1-1/3 CUPS ALL-PURPOSE FLOUR

3/4 TEASPOON BAKING SODA

1 EGG

1 TABLESPOON VANILLA EXTRACT

1/3 CUP BUTTERMILK

1 CUP BUTTERSCOTCH CHIPS

Preheat oven to 350F (175C). Grease a 13" x 9" baking pan. In a large bowl, cream together brown sugar and butter or margarine until light and fluffy. Add oats, flour, baking soda, egg, vanilla and buttermilk beating thoroughly. Fold in butterscotch chips. Spread into prepared pan. Bake 20 to 25 minutes until golden brown and a wooden pick inserted in center comes out barely moist with crumbs. Set on a wire rack and cool in pan. Cut in 32 bars.

Oatmeal Cookie Bars

Chewy, fruit-filled bars that are a snap to bake.

2/3 CUP BUTTER OR MARGARINE,
    SOFTENED

1-1/4 CUPS PACKED DARK BROWN SUGAR

3 TEASPOONS VANILLA EXTRACT

1 EGG

3/4 CUP ALL-PURPOSE FLOUR

1-1/4 CUPS ROLLED OATS

1/2 CUP DARK RAISINS

1/2 CUP GOLDEN RAISINS

1/2 CUP SEMISWEET CHOCOLATE CHIPS

1/2 CUP MILK CHOCOLATE CHIPS

Preheat oven to 350F (175C). Grease a 13" x 9" baking pan. In a large bowl, cream together butter or margarine and brown sugar until light and fluffy. Add vanilla and egg, blending well. Stir in flour. Add oats, mixing thoroughly. Fold in raisins and semisweet and milk chocolate chips. Spread into prepared pan. Bake 18 to 23 minutes. Set on a wire rack and cool in pan. Cut in 32 bars.

Variation: Decrease vanilla extract to 1 teaspoon and add 1 teaspoon orange juice and 1 teaspoon grated orange peel. Substitute 1 cup vanilla chips for raisins and semisweet and milk chocolate chips.

Chocolate Wafer Bars

How could something so simple (only five ingredients) be so delicious?

2 CUPS LIGHTLY PACKED CHOCOLATE
    WAFER CRUMBS

1 (14-OZ.) CAN SWEETENED CONDENSED
    MILK

1 TABLESPOON VANILLA EXTRACT

1/2 CUP WHITE CHOCOLATE CHIPS

1/2 CUP MILK CHOCOLATE CHIPS

POWDERED SUGAR

Preheat oven to 350F (175C). Grease a 9-inch-square baking pan. In a large bowl, blend together chocolate wafer crumbs and condensed milk. Stir in vanilla, then white chocolate chips and milk chocolate chips. Spread into prepared pan. Bake 25 to 30 minutes. Set on a wire rack and cool in pan. Dust with powdered sugar. Cut in 25 bars.

California Granola Blondies

The wholesome goodness of granola and tangy touch of orange give these easy blondies the California twist.

1/2 CUP BUTTER OR MARGARINE

2 CUPS PACKED DARK BROWN SUGAR

1 EGG

1/4 CUP FRESH ORANGE JUICE

1 TEASPOON GRATED ORANGE PEEL

1 TEASPOON VANILLA EXTRACT

1-1/2 CUPS ALL-PURPOSE FLOUR

1 TEASPOON BAKING POWDER

1-1/2 CUPS GRANOLA

Preheat oven to 350F (175C). Grease a 13" x 9" baking pan. In a medium saucepan over low heat, melt butter or margarine. Stir in brown sugar and mix well. Remove from heat and let cool slightly. In a medium bowl, beat egg, orange juice, orange peel and vanilla, blending well. Add brown sugar mixture and blend thoroughly. Stir in flour and baking powder. Add granola and stir thoroughly. Spread into prepared pan. Bake 25 to 30 minutes, or until a wooden pick inserted in center comes out barely moist with crumbs. Set on a wire rack and cool in pan. Cut in 30 bars.

Peanut Butter Brownie Cups

Kids will love these chewy peanut-butter-filled brownie cupcakes. Different colored cupcake foils will add a festive touch to this unique birthday party dessert.

1 CUP UNSALTED BUTTER OR MARGARINE

4 OUNCES UNSWEETENED CHOCOLATE

2 CUPS GRANULATED SUGAR

3 EGGS

1 TABLESPOON VANILLA EXTRACT

1 CUP ALL-PURPOSE FLOUR

12 BITE-SIZE CHOCOLATE-PEANUT-BUTTER
   CUPS

POWDERED SUGAR

Preheat oven to 350F (175C). Line 12 standard muffin cups (2-1/2-inch diameter) with foil baking cups. In a large saucepan, heat butter or margarine over moderately low heat until half melted. Add chocolate stirring until completely melted. Remove from heat and stir in sugar. Then beat in eggs, one at a time, until mixture is shiny. Add vanilla, flour and mix until well blended. Spoon 1/4 cup batter into prepared muffin cups. Gently press a bite-size chocolate-peanut-butter cup into center of each. Bake for 30 minutes. Dust with powdered sugar and let cool before removing from pans. Makes 12 brownie cupcakes.

Perfect Penuche Bars

Gooey, chewy chocolatey coconut bars that are so good they'll disappear faster than it takes to bake a batch!

BROWN SUGAR CRUST

1/2 CUP BUTTER OR MARGARINE, SOFTENED

1/2 CUP PACKED DARK BROWN SUGAR

1 CUP ALL-PURPOSE FLOUR

2 TABLESPOONS MILK

❖

CHOCOLATE-COCONUT TOPPING

2 EGGS

1 CUP PACKED DARK BROWN SUGAR

1 TABLESPOON VANILLA EXTRACT

2 TABLESPOONS ALL-PURPOSE FLOUR

1/2 TEASPOON BAKING POWDER

1-1/3 CUPS FLAKED COCONUT

1 CUP CHOPPED PECANS

3/4 CUP SEMISWEET CHOCOLATE CHIPS

Brown Sugar Crust

Preheat oven to 325F (165C). Grease a 9-inch-square baking pan. In a medium bowl, cream butter or margarine and brown sugar. Mix in flour, then milk. Pat evenly into prepared pan. Bake about 20 minutes, until a light golden brown. Remove from oven and place on a wire rack. Maintain oven temperature. Prepare Chocolate-Coconut Topping. Spread evenly over crust and return to oven. Bake 20 minutes, until golden brown. Set on a wire rack and cool in pan. Cut in 36 bars.

Chocolate-Coconut Topping

In a large bowl, combine eggs, brown sugar and vanilla; blend thoroughly. Stir in flour and baking powder; mix well. Stir in coconut, pecans and chocolate chips.

Upside-Down Coconut Blondies

*A couple of additions to standard yellow cake mix turn
out irresistible dessert treats–flavored with almond and coconut.*

1 (18.25-OZ.) BOX YELLOW CAKE MIX

2 EGG WHITES

3/4 CUP BUTTERMILK

3/4 CUP COLD WATER

1/3 CUP VEGETABLE OIL

1/2 TABLESPOON VANILLA EXTRACT

1 TEASPOON ALMOND EXTRACT

2/3 CUP ALL-PURPOSE FLOUR

2/3 CUP PACKED DARK BROWN SUGAR

1 CUP FLAKED COCONUT

1/2 CUP PECANS (OPTIONAL)

1 CUP BUTTER OR MARGARINE, MELTED

Preheat oven to 350F (175C). Grease a 13" x 9" baking pan. In a large bowl, combine cake mix, egg whites, buttermilk, water, oil, vanilla and almond extracts; blend on low speed until moistened. Mix at medium speed for two minutes; set aside. In a medium bowl, combine flour, brown sugar, coconut and nuts, if desired. Pour melted butter or margarine over top, blending thoroughly. Spread evenly into prepared pan. Pour cake batter over coconut mixture. Bake 32 to 35 minutes, or until a wooden pick inserted in center comes out barely moist with crumbs. Turn upside down immediately on a foil rectangle. Then set on a wire rack to cool. Cut in 35 bars.

Caramel-Chocolate Chewies

Caramels and chocolate chips turn ordinary German chocolate cake into an extraordinary chewy dessert.

1 (14-OZ.) PACKAGE CARAMELS

2/3 CUP EVAPORATED MILK

1 (18-OZ.) BOX GERMAN CHOCOLATE
CAKE MIX

3/4 CUP BUTTER OR MARGARINE,
SOFTENED

1 CUP CHOPPED PECANS

1 (12-OZ.) PACKAGE SEMISWEET
CHOCOLATE CHIPS

Preheat oven to 350F (175C). Grease a 13" x 9" baking pan. In a small saucepan over low heat, melt caramels with 1/3 cup evaporated milk. Remove from heat. In a large bowl, combine cake mix, remaining evaporated milk and butter or margarine. Mix until cake mixture holds together. Stir in pecans. Press half of cake mixture into prepared pan and bake 6 minutes. Remove from oven and sprinkle chocolate chips evenly on top. Pour melted caramel mixture over chocolate. Return to oven and bake 15 to 18 minutes. Set on wire rack and cool in pan. Cut in 48 bars.

Cinnamon Coffee Bars

A delicious flavor combination of coffee and cinnamon, makes perfect, iced bite-size treats for breakfast, breaks or midnight snacks.

1/4 CUP BUTTER OR MARGARINE, SOFTENED

1 CUP PACKED DARK BROWN SUGAR

1 EGG

1/2 CUP STRONG HOT COFFEE

1-1/2 CUPS ALL-PURPOSE FLOUR

1 TEASPOON BAKING POWDER

1/4 TEASPOON BAKING SODA

3/4 TEASPOON GROUND CINNAMON

3/4 CUP RAISINS

1/2 CUP CHOPPED NUTS (OPTIONAL)

❖

CREAM ICING

1-1/2 CUPS POWDERED SUGAR, SIFTED

1 TEASPOON VANILLA EXTRACT

2 TO 3 TABLESPOONS WHIPPING CREAM

Preheat oven to 350F (175C). Grease a 13" x 9" baking pan. In a large bowl, combine butter or margarine, brown sugar and egg; mix until light and fluffy. Add coffee; blend thoroughly. Stir together flour, baking powder, baking soda and cinnamon; blend into coffee mixture. Fold in raisins and nuts, if desired. Spread into prepared pan. Bake 18 to 20 minutes, or until a wooden pick inserted in center comes out barely moist with crumbs. Prepare Cream Icing. While still warm, frost bars. Set on a wire rack and cool in pan. Cut in 24 bars.

Cream Icing
Combine all ingredients, blending until smooth and creamy.

Chewy Caramel-Coconut Brownies

Chewy caramel-smothered brownies taste great and are quick to bake!

1 PACKAGE BROWNIE MIX (MAKES 24 TO
   36 SQUARES)
20 CARAMELS
3 TABLESPOONS MILK
1 CUP CHOPPED PECANS
1/2 CUP SHREDDED COCONUT

Preheat oven to temperature indicated on packaged brownie mix. Prepare and bake brownies according to box directions for either cakelike or fudge brownies. Set on a wire rack and cool in pan, but do not cut. In a small saucepan over medium-low heat, stir caramels and milk until melted and smooth. Spread evenly over uncut brownies. Sprinkle with pecans and coconut. Cut in 24 to 36 squares and serve.

Gingersnap Macadamia Nut Brownies

A delicious combination that's a snap to make!

1 BOX BROWNIE MIX (MAKES 24 TO 36
   SQUARES)
20 (ABOUT 1-1/2 CUP) GINGERSNAPS,
   CRUMBLED
1 CUP MACADAMIA NUTS

Preheat oven to temperature indicated on packaged brownie mix. Prepare brownie batter according to box directions for either cakelike or fudge brownies. Stir crumbled gingersnaps into batter. Spread into prepared baking pan. Sprinkle with macadamia nuts and bake according to directions. Set on a wire rack and cool in pan. Cut in 24 to 36 squares.

Berry Almond Brownies

A flavor-filled cream cheese topping makes these rich brownies a royal treat!

1 PACKAGE BROWNIE MIX (MAKES 24 TO
   36 SQUARES)
3 OUNCES CREAM CHEESE, SOFTENED
2 TABLESPOONS SUGAR
2 TABLESPOONS BUTTER OR MARGARINE,
   SOFTENED
1 EGG
1 TABLESPOON ALL-PURPOSE FLOUR
1/2 TEASPOON ALMOND EXTRACT
1/3 CUP SEEDLESS RASPBERRY OR
   BLACKBERRY JAM
SLIVERED ALMONDS (OPTIONAL)

Preheat oven to temperature indicated on packaged brownie mix. Prepare brownie batter according to box directions for either cakelike or fudge brownies. Spread batter into prepared pan. Set aside. In a medium bowl, beat together cream cheese, sugar, butter or margarine, egg, flour and almond extract until smooth. Pour evenly over brownie batter. Drop teaspoon-sized dollops of jam over top. Bake 35 to 40 minutes, or until lightly browned. Set on a wire rack and cool in pan. Cut in 24 to 36 squares. Garnish with almond slivers, if desired.

Hint of Mint Brownies

Two simple additions to an ordinary brownie mix makes these extraordinarily good delights!

1 PACKAGE BROWNIE MIX (MAKES 24 TO
   36 SQUARES)
1 CUP CHOCOLATE MINT CHIPS
1/2 TEASPOON PEPPERMINT EXTRACT

Preheat oven to temperature indicated on packaged brownie mix. Prepare brownie batter according to box directions for either cakelike or fudge brownies. Stir mint chocolate chips and peppermint extract into batter. Spread into prepared pan. Bake according to box directions. Set on a wire rack and cool in pan. Cut in 24 to 36 squares.

Peanut Butter and Chocolate Brownies

Kids will love the crunchy candy surprises in these chocolatey brownies.

1 PACKAGE BROWNIE MIX (MAKES 24 TO
   36 SQUARES)
1/2 CUP CANDY-COATED CHOCOLATES
1/2 CUP CANDY-COATED PEANUT BUTTER
   CHOCOLATES

Preheat oven to temperature indicated on packaged brownie mix. Prepare brownie batter according to box directions for either cakelike or fudge brownies. Stir candy-coated chocolates and candy-coated peanut butter chocolates into batter. Spread into prepared pan. Bake according to box directions. Set on a wire rack and cool in pan. Cut in 24 to 36 squares.

Rocky Road Brownies

For a doubly-delicious delight, serve with rocky road ice cream.

1 PACKAGE BROWNIE MIX (MAKES 24 TO
   36 SQUARES)
1 CUP MINIATURE MARSHMALLOWS
1/2 CUP SEMISWEET CHOCOLATE CHIPS
CHOCOLATE SYRUP

Preheat oven to temperature indicated on packaged brownie mix. Prepare brownie batter according to box directions for either cakelike or fudge brownies. Spread batter into prepared pan. Sprinkle with marshmallows and chocolate chips. Bake according to box directions. Set on a wire rack and cool in pan. Cut in 24 to 36 squares. Drizzle chocolate syrup over top before serving.

Minty Good Brownies

The perfect after-dinner finisher—serve with ice-cold milk and hot coffee.

1 PACKAGE BROWNIE MIX (MAKES 24 TO
   36 SQUARES)

1/2 CUP BUTTER OR MARGARINE,
   SOFTENED

2 CUPS POWDERED SUGAR

3 TABLESPOONS GREEN CRÈME DE
   MENTHE

❖

CHOCOLATE GLAZE

1 CUP SEMISWEET CHOCOLATE CHIPS

6 TABLESPOONS BUTTER OR MARGARINE,
   SOFTENED

CHOCOLATE CANDY MINT WAFERS,
   COARSELY CHOPPED

Preheat oven to temperature indicated on packaged brownie mix. Prepare and bake brownies according to box directions for either cakelike or fudge brownies. Set on a wire rack and cool in pan but do not cut. In a medium bowl, beat butter or margarine, powdered sugar and crème de menthe until smooth. Spread over baked brownies. Prepare Chocolate Glaze. Pour over crème de menthe layer and spread evenly. Cool until glaze sets. Sprinkle with chopped mint wafers. Cut in 24 to 36 squares.

Chocolate Glaze

In a small saucepan over low heat, stir chocolate chips and butter or margarine until smooth. Remove from heat and allow to cool.

Chocolate Cookie Brownies

Why serve plain ol' cookies and milk when this freshly-baked version can be made in minutes?

1 PACKAGE BROWNIE MIX (MAKES 24 TO
   36 SQUARES)
15 CHOCOLATE SANDWICH COOKIES,
   CRUMBLED
CHOCOLATE SYRUP

Preheat oven to temperature indicated on packaged brownie mix. Prepare brownies according to box directions for either cakelike or fudge brownies. Bake 15 minutes then remove and sprinkle crumbled cookies on top. Return to oven and bake an additional 15 to 20 minutes. Set on a wire rack and cool in pan. Drizzle chocolate syrup over brownies before serving. Cut in 24 to 36 squares.

Chocolate Graham Cracker Bars

Tasty, no-fuss treats–perfect for lunch boxes.

2 CUPS GRAHAM CRACKER CRUMBS
1 CUP SEMISWEET CHOCOLATE CHIPS
3/4 CUP FLAKED COCONUT
1 (14-OZ.) CAN SWEETENED CONDENSED
   MILK
1/2 CUP CHOPPED NUTS (OPTIONAL)

Preheat oven to 350F (175C). Grease an 8-inch-square baking pan. In a medium bowl, combine graham cracker crumbs, chocolate chips, coconut and condensed milk. Mix thoroughly. Spoon into prepared pan. Bake 25 to 30 minutes. Set on a wire rack and cool in pan. Sprinkle nuts evenly over top, if desired. Cut in 16 squares.

Caramel Confections

Delicious, caramel-oat bars finished off with fudge topping.

2 CUPS ROLLED OATS

1/2 CUP PACKED DARK BROWN SUGAR

1/2 CUP BUTTER OR MARGARINE

1/4 CUP DARK CORN SYRUP

2 TEASPOONS VANILLA EXTRACT

2 CUPS SEMISWEET CHOCOLATE CHIPS

1/4 CUP CHOPPED NUTS

Preheat oven to 400F (205C). Grease a 9-inch-square baking pan. In a medium bowl, mix oats and brown sugar. In a small saucepan, melt butter or margarine with corn syrup and vanilla. Pour over oat mixture, stirring until well blended. Spread evenly into prepared pan. Bake 8 to 10 minutes. Do not overbake–cookies will be bubbly when done. Set on a wire rack and cool in pan. Melt chocolate chips and spread over bars; sprinkle with nuts. Cut in 32 bars.

English Toffee Bars

A delicious candylike toffee that's simple to make.

15 GRAHAM CRACKERS (2-1/2 X 2-1/2-INCHES)

1 CUP PACKED DARK BROWN SUGAR

1 CUP BUTTER (MARGARINE NOT RECOMMENDED)

1 (6-OZ.) PACKAGE MILK CHOCOLATE CHIPS

1/4 CUP CHOPPED PECANS OR WALNUTS

Preheat oven to 400F (205C). Line a 9-inch-square baking pan with foil. Grease foil. Cover bottom of foiled pan evenly with graham crackers. In a medium saucepan over medium-high heat, combine brown sugar and butter and bring to a boil. Remove from heat and pour over graham crackers. Bake 5 minutes. Remove from oven and sprinkle with chocolate chips. As soon as chocolate chips are soft, spread evenly over crust. Sprinkle with nuts. Chill at least 30 minutes, or until chocolate is set. Cut in 16 bars.

Metric Conversion Chart

Comparison to Metric Measure

When You Know	Symbol	Multiply By	To Find	Symbol
teaspoons	tsp	5.0	milliliters	ml
tablespoons	tbsp	15.0	milliliters	ml
fluid ounces	fl. oz.	30.0	milliliters	ml
cups	c	0.24	liters	l
pints	pt.	0.47	liters	l
quarts	qt.	0.95	liters	l
ounces	oz.	28.0	grams	g
pounds	lb.	0.45	kilograms	kg
Fahrenheit	F	5/9 (after subtracting 32)	Celsius	C

Liquid Measure to Milliliters

1/4 teaspoon	=	1.25 milliliters
1/2 teaspoon	=	2.5 milliliters
3/4 teaspoon	=	3.75 milliliters
1 teaspoon	=	5.0 milliliters
1-1/4 teaspoons	=	6.25 milliliters
1-1/2 teaspoons	=	7.5 milliliters
1-3/4 teaspoons	=	8.75 milliliters
2 teaspoons	=	10.0 milliliters
1 tablespoon	=	15.0 milliliters
2 tablespoons	=	30.0 milliliters

Fahrenheit to Celsius

F	C
200—205	95
220—225	105
245—250	120
275	135
300—305	150
325—330	165
345—350	175
370—375	190
400—405	205
425—430	220
445—450	230
470—475	245
500	260

Liquid Measure to Liters

1/4 cup	=	0.06 liters
1/2 cup	=	0.12 liters
3/4 cup	=	0.18 liters
1 cup	=	0.24 liters
1-1/4 cups	=	0.3 liters
1-1/2 cups	=	0.36 liters
2 cups	=	0.48 liters
2-1/2 cups	=	0.6 liters
3 cups	=	0.72 liters
3-1/2 cups	=	0.84 liters
4 cups	=	0.96 liters
4-1/2 cups	=	1.08 liters
5 cups	=	1.2 liters
5-1/2 cups	=	1.32 liters

Index